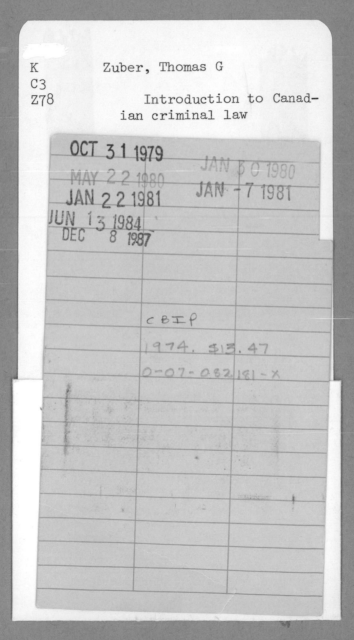

introduction to CANADIAN CRIMINAL LAW

Thomas G. Zuber
Justice of the Supreme Court of Ontario

McGRAW-HILL RYERSON LIMITED

Toronto   Montreal   New York   London   Sydney
Johannesburg   Mexico   Panama   Düsseldorf
Singapore   São Paulo   Kuala Lumpur   New Delhi

Introduction to Canadian Criminal Law

ISBN 0-07-082181-x

2 3 4 5 6 7 8 9 10   D   3 2 1 0 9 8 7 6 5

Printed and bound in Canada

CONTENTS

PREFACE

In recent years there has been a remarkable increase in the number of students in secondary schools who are electing to study some form of law. In most instances a general textbook is used with occasional additional material provided by teachers. Mr. W. H. Jennings and I are gratified that one such general text is *Canadian Law* (McGraw-Hill Ryerson 1972).

In these texts, criminal law can necessarily be dealt with only in a general way. There seems, however, to be a great interest amongst students in the criminal law and a resulting demand for a more specialized text. Toward that end this small book has been prepared and is intended to be a companion or supplementary volume to the more general texts. Certain general concepts and terms which are dealt with in the general texts are not here dealt with or explained again. The reader who is unfamiliar with Unit One of *Canadian Law* or one of the other general textbooks will find that an occasional reference to a good dictionary may be necessary.

The purpose of this book is to provide the student with a somewhat deeper and wider view of the criminal law. It is hoped as well to demonstrate the problems in the formulation of the criminal law, its interpretation and administration. As a result, the student may well become more appreciative and more constructively critical of the criminal law and its administration.

T.G.Z.

I

THE NATURE OF CRIMINAL LAW

In a general way we are all familiar with the terms "crime" and "criminal law". Our reaction to the terms may vary from one of great interest in a highly dramatic criminal trial to a feeling of revulsion towards a particularly sordid crime. Crime has been defined as an act or omission which is prohibited and punished by the State for the purpose of restraining antisocial behaviour. This definition, however, leads to further questions. What types of acts are prohibited and punished? Who defines them and prescribes the punishment? What characteristics distinguish criminal conduct from conduct that is not regarded as criminal? We must look further for the answers to these questions.

HISTORY

The basis of our criminal law is to be found in the common law of England. Early English courts through case law developed concepts of those basic crimes, e.g., murder, rape, treason, assault, theft, which still form the core of our criminal law. In formulating these basic concepts, the common law courts drew upon the universally accepted moral values of the community, or those principles necessary for the maintenance of authority.

The modern law of torts (civil wrongs) deals with compensation as between individuals for wrongs which constitute a wrong against the community as a whole. In Anglo-Saxon times (449 A.D.-1066 A.D.), however, there was no clear-cut distinction between the law of tort and crime. Legal action was always initiated by the person wronged or his relatives, and compensation was awarded and punishment inflicted in the same proceeding. The idea of a crime as an offence against the State was recognized in that punishment was inflicted on the wrongdoer, but the primary object was to compensate the victim. Faced with a private accusation of crime, an accused in those days might defend himself in several ways.

(a) Trial by Ordeal

This form of trial was basically an appeal to supernatural powers to assist in the decision-making process. An accused person would subject himself to some form of ordeal and if he passed the ordeal successfully he was deemed innocent. The ordeals took a variety of forms depending on the particular

1

locality. It would appear that the ordeals themselves predated Christianity, but were so deeply rooted in the customs of the people that the Christian Church accepted the ordeals and surrounded them with Christian ceremony. In a typical ordeal, a priest called upon a pool of water to receive the accused who, if he sank, was declared to have come clean from the ordeal. If he floated, he was held guilty. Another ordeal involved a hot iron being given to an accused at Mass who would carry the hot iron a distance of nine feet. His hand would then be bound up and after three days the bandages removed. If the wound was unclean the accused was considered guilty. In the ordeal of the cursed morsel, the accused was obliged to swallow a certain type of morsel, sometimes a feather inside food. If the accused was able to swallow it successfully he was innocent; if he choked he was guilty. The number and types of ordeals varied considerably.

(b) Trial by Compurgation or Wager of Law

This type of trial consisted of the accused person swearing an oath to the truth as to his innocence. The oath was taken by the person involved, aided by oath helpers or compurgators, often eleven or twelve in number. These oath helpers were not witnesses who swore to their knowledge of the facts in issue; they simply swore that the oath taken by the principal party was a good oath and they believed it. Essentially, the compurgators or oath helpers were character witnesses. This form of trial was discouraged in criminal trials, but continued to have a place in civil trials. Despite the fact that it fell into disuse with the growth of the jury system, the trial by wager of law lingered in the common law system and was not abolished in England until 1833.

(c) Trial by Battle

This method of trial appears to have been introduced into England by the conquering Normans, though it is possible that the Danes may have brought it to England as early as the tenth century. This method of trial involved actual combat by the parties to the lawsuit or their champions. Trial by battle was available only in private proceedings and was not available where the accused person had been accused by a grand jury or where the Crown was a party to the dispute. Trial by battle was basically a form of ordeal and it was thought in Christian times that God would intervene to defend the right. The victor in the battle was the victor in the legal dispute. Despite the fact that this manner of trial became obsolete with the evolution of the jury sysem, it was not abolished until the nineteenth century.

Public Prosecution for Crime

The Anglo-Saxon kings and early Norman kings, threatened, as they

THE LAST TRIAL BY BATTLE

In 1817, Abraham Thornton was charged with the murder of Mary Ashford. He was tried before a jury in Warwickshire, England, and acquitted. But there were some who believed Thornton guilty; William Ashford, brother of the deceased girl, was one of them. Ashford continued to seek satisfaction, but there was little public authorities could do, even had they wanted to, because in those times there was no provision for an appeal in criminal cases.

Ashford, with great perseverance and with the aid of his resourceful solicitors, charged Thornton with the murder of his sister by private accusation. For centuries the public authorities had assumed the duty of prosecuting criminal cases, but the right of private accusation, though dormant, was still alive. Strangely enough, it was no answer that Thornton had already been acquitted in a prior trial. The two proceedings were quite separate. In 1817, Thornton again faced a charge of murdering Mary Ashford. Thornton, in response to the charge, replied, "Not guilty, I am ready to defend the same by my body." He then removed an ancient medieval gauntlet from his hand and threw it to the floor. By these words and actions he had elected trial by battle. Since the right to launch a criminal prosecution by private accusation had survived, so had the right to trial by battle. Faced with this development, Ashford lost heart. The case was adjourned and Ashford failed to appear. Thornton, the victor by default, was released. In 1819, trial by battle and criminal prosecutions by private accusation were abolished by the English Parliament.

usually were, from within and without, were kept thoroughly occupied maintaining their position on the throne. They had little extra effort to devote to helping their subjects in the administration of justice. By the twelfth century, great progress had been made in the establishment of a strong central government in England and the community became more settled. The monarchy was therefore able to turn its attention to the suppression of minor disorders and at this point there began a transition wherein the Crown began to assume the responsibility for the criminal law. This gradual process was accomplished in two ways:

(1) The King's Peace

Cases in which the Crown had always been interested were described as "pleas of the Crown" and in the beginning were fairly limited in scope. They involved infringements of the king's property and monetary rights, cases involving injury to the king in respect of his royal office, e.g., refusing military service, treason, etc., and lastly, cases involving a breach of the king's peace. Shortly after the Norman Conquest (1066 A.D.), the concept of the king's peace was local, personal, and generally confined to the specific area where the king was residing. Acts of violence within the area covered by the king's peace were considered an affront to the Crown and were accordingly dealt with as public wrongs. Gradually the king's peace grew to cover the entire country at all times, and any serious disorder invariably involved a breach of the king's peace.

(2) The Statutes of Clarendon and Northampton

The Normans also introduced a more systematic criminal administration. In the twelfth century, King Henry II put certain offences in a special category by the statutes of Clarendon and Northampton. These statutes provided that twelve men in every hundred (a territorial division) must present to the Justice of Assize all the serious crimes that were committed in that territory when the Justice of Assize came to the area. The duty of this group was to investigate and to bring criminal cases to the attention of the judges so that a trial might be held. It was not their duty to adjudicate upon guilt or innocence. This group became known as the grand jury. With the passage of time the investigation aspect of its work was performed by the police, but it remained for the grand jury to say whether or not a person would be indicted (accused in writing) by the grand jury and put on trial.

Crown Responsibility

The Statutes of Clarendon and Northampton did not abolish any private rights that might arise from the offences, but the State took upon itself the duty of dealing with the gravest offences. Eventually the administration of criminal law became entirely the responsibility of the Crown and today it is a distinctive characteristic of criminal law that cases are conducted by public officers in the name of the Crown. The very names of the cases reflect this concept; criminal cases are styled as *Regina* or *The Queen* v. *The Accused,* whoever he or she may be.

Trial By Jury

Once an accused was presented or indicted by the presenting, or grand, jury, the trial took place. In the early days, the trial was customarily by ordeal. In 1215 Pope Innocent III forbade the clergy to perform any religious ceremonies in connection with the ordeals. As a result, the ordeal was abolished in substance since without the attendant religious aspect the ordeal lost its supernatural quality. The itinerant Justices trying criminal cases were put in a position of having to find some method whereby the alleged criminal could be tried. The judges persuaded the alleged criminal to "put himself upon his country", i.e., abide by the decision of twelve jurors. In the early stages the division between the presenting jury and the trying jury who decided guilt or innocence was ill-defined and the juries may have been the same. Even if they were not the same, some of the jurors on the presenting jury may have been members of the trying jury or, as it ultimately came to be called, the petit jury. Ultimately the two juries became separate and the system became well-established. By degrees, trial by jury became the only method of trial.

PRINCIPLES OF CRIMINAL LAW

It is generally considered that a crime consists of two elements—an objective element that embraces the act or conduct and a subjective element which includes the mental state of the accused. For example:

> Smith fires his gun killing Jones. The objective element is the act of firing the gun. The subjective element is the state of Smith's mind. Was the firing accidental or deliberate? If deliberate, did Smith intend to kill, to warn, to frighten, etc.?

Anglo-Saxon law was not concerned with the subjective aspect and if a man caused the death of another he had to answer for the result regardless of whether he intended it or not. As the common law of England developed, no doubt influenced by the Church, which looked for a mental element in its concept of sin, there was increasing acceptance of the notion that criminal intent was necessary for a crime. Criminal intent is frequently referred to as *mens rea* or guilty mind. The concept of *mens rea*, while a necessary element in most offences, varies with respect to the different offences. A different type of intent is required for murder than for theft, for example. A consideration of the doctrine of *mens rea* in detail requires a consideration of the offence involved.

For many fairly simple crimes, the guilty intent required is simply the intent to commit the forbidden act. For example:

> if Andrews strikes Burns intentionally, it is an assault; if Andrews strikes Burns accidentally, it is not intentional and therefore not an assault.

Some crimes are more complex and are defined to require a more complicated state of mind. Many of these crimes (e.g., murder) require an intentional act with a further intent to produce a specific result. For example:

> if Andrews strikes Burns intending only to blacken his eye and kills Burns, he will not be guilty of murder; while Andrews intended to strike Burns, he did not intend to kill.

This type of intent is frequently described as "specific intent".

In modern times, however, in some specific instances Parliament has been obliged to return to the concept of criminal responsibility without guilty intent. In such instances, (e.g., driving while impaired by alcohol) Parliament has found it necessary to prohibit certain conduct and attach to it criminal sanctions despite the absence of a guilty intent by the accused.

Presumption of Innocence

It is apparent that in the early forms of trial, the accused could hardly be said to be presumed innocent. The accusation obliged the accused to submit to an ordeal, battle, or wager of law. With the change in the method of trial to trial by jury, the duty fell upon the prosecution to adduce evidence that the accused was guilty. It is likely that the burden of proof was not a particularly stringent one in the beginning, since all or some of the jurors had actual knowledge of the facts, having been members of the presenting jury. Gradually the courts evolved the doctrine that the accused was presumed innocent until the prosecution proved his guilt beyond a reasonable doubt. The obligation to prove guilt beyond a reasonable doubt sometimes results in the acquittal of the guilty, but it is one of the principles of our law that it is preferable that some guilty escape rather than risk convicting an innocent man.

C-1

Woolmington was charged with the murder of his wife. The evidence was clear that Woolmington had shot his wife. His explanation, however, was that the shooting was an accident. The trial judge instructed the jury that if they were satisfied that the killing was caused by Woolmington, he should be found guilty of murder unless accident was satisfactorily proved by the prisoner. Woolmington was convicted and appealed. The House of Lords reversed the decision in this case, saying:

> **Throughout the web of the English Criminal Law one golden thread is always to be seen, that it is the duty of the prosecution to prove the prisoner's guilt (subject to insanity or any statutory exception). If at the end of and on the whole of the case there is a reasonable doubt created by the evidence given by either**

the prosecution or the prisoner as to whether the prisoner killed the deceased with malicious intention, the prosecution has not made out the case and the prisoner is entitled to an acquittal. No matter what the charge or where the trial, the principle that the prosecution must prove the guilt of the prisoner is part of the common law of England and no attempt to whittle it down can be entertained.

   (a) What important principle of criminal law is evident in the reversal?

   (b) Explain in what way the trial judge was not following this principle.

   (c) Does the standard described by the House of Lords ever lead to the acquittal of the guilty and if so, how can this be justified?

The Criminal Law in Canada

The law of crime was developed by the common law system. The criminal law inherited by the various Canadian provinces from England was essentially a case law system with slight modifications by English statutes. For a time, each province was free to modify by statute the criminal law that it had inherited, and a few such statutes were passed. In 1867, the first four provinces were united into a single country and jurisdiction over criminal law was assigned to the federal parliament.

The Criminal Code

Meanwhile, in England the idea of codifying the criminal law was gaining in popularity. In 1838, the first criminal law commissioners were appointed to draft a criminal code, and in 1878 the English draft code was produced but was not passed by the English Parliament despite two attempts. In Canada, the draft code found favour. With a few minor changes, the draft code was passed by the Canadian Parliament in 1892, received Royal assent the same year, and came into force on July 1, 1893. The passage of this code represented a great improvement in the state of the criminal law but the code did not abolish all common law offences or deal with the pre-confederation provincial statutes. In 1953, when the Canadian Criminal Code was revised, offences contrary to common law, English statutes, and pre-confederation criminal statutes were abolished.

However, the Criminal Code did not abolish the common law dealing with defences. Section 7, subjection (3) of the Criminal Code provides:

Every rule and principle of the common law that renders any circumstance a justification or excuse for an act or a defence to a charge continues in force and applies in respect of proceed-

ings for an offence under this Act or any other Act of the Parliament of Canada, except in so far as they are altered by or are inconsistent with this Act or any other Act of the Parliament of Canada.

While the Criminal Code contains most of the criminal law of Canada in the popular sense, i.e., provisions dealing with robbery, theft, murder, etc., it does not contain all of our criminal law.

Other Criminal Legislation

It has been necessary for the federal parliament to incorporate criminal provisions into other legislative enactments and indeed prohibit new types of conduct. Important criminal legislation is therefore to be found in many other Acts of Parliament, e.g., the Juvenile Delinquents Act, the Combines Investigations Act, the Narcotic Control Act, the Official Secrets Act, and others.

Provincial and Municipal Powers

While the provincial legislatures cannot pass criminal law in the strict sense of the term, they are entitled to provide punishment by fine, penalty, or imprisonment to enforce provincial laws. The provinces are given jurisdiction to legislate over a wide variety of subjects by section 92 of the British North America Act, and it is obvious that in order to enforce compliance with their own laws the Provincial Legislatures must have enforcement procedures. Provincial legislation which provides for punishment in the event of noncompliance is not, strictly speaking, regarded as criminal law, although in many cases the fines are large and the periods of imprisonment long. For example,

> the provinces have statutes which regulate the ownership and operation of motor vehicles, the sale of beer and liquor. Fines and/or jail terms are provided for breaches of these statutes.

Prosecutions of those in breach of provincial statutes are usually conducted by public authorities and in a manner similar to ordinary criminal proceedings. Offences against provincial law are sometimes described as *quasi*-criminal and many of the legal principles governing these prosecutions are taken from the criminal law.

The provincial legislatures in turn have delegated some of their authority to municipalities and as a result, cities, towns, counties, etc., are entitled to pass by-laws governing the licensing of businesses, the regulation of traffic within their boundaries, building codes, etc. The municipalities are also entitled to enforce compliance with their laws by the imposition of fines or even terms of imprisonment. Again, while municipal by-laws are not, strictly speaking, criminal laws, their enforcement is in many ways similar to the ordinary criminal process.

New Crimes

When the federal parliament assumed exclusive jurisdiction over the criminal law in 1867, the classification of crimes was not frozen for all time. The power of the federal government extends to the definition of new crimes. With changing times and new problems, new laws have been passed covering such things as the operation of motor vehicles, price fixing, etc. In 1972, parliament reacted to the rash of aircraft hijackings and added to the Criminal Code several sections dealing with the problem. The principal section is as follows:

> **76.1   Every one who, unlawfully, by force or threat thereof, or by any other form of intimidation, seizes or exercises control of an aircraft with intent**
> **(a) to cause any person on board the aircraft to be confined or imprisoned against his will,**
> **(b) to cause any person on board the aircraft to be transported against his will to any place other than the next scheduled place of landing of the aircraft,**
> **(c) to hold any person on board the aircraft for ransom or to service against his will, or**
> **(d) to cause the aircraft to deviate in a material respect from its flight plan,**
> **is guilty of an indictable offence and is liable to imprisonment for life.**

The Many Faces of Crime

The term "crime" does not cover a single area of activity or even a variety of areas covered by some unifying theory. Crime is made up of many types of conduct which include stealing a car for a joyride, the sale of narcotics, murder, conspiracy to fix prices. Even the terms themselves contain a wide range of meaning. For example, a mercy killing and a hired assassination are both described as murder.

Different times and problems cause lawmakers to classify certain conduct as criminal. Subsequent generations may have difficulty in understanding what led society in one era to classify certain conduct as criminal. For example, one wonders what conditions led to the creation of the following specific offences which still appear in the Criminal Code.

> **Section 154:**
> **Every male person who, being the owner or master of, or employed on board a vessel, engaged in the carriage of passengers for hire, seduces, or by threats or by the exercise of his authority, has illicit sexual intercourse on board the vessel with a female passenger is guilty of an indictable offence and is liable to imprisonment for two years.**

CRIME IN CANADA, 1970

| | | Persons charged | | | |
| | | Adults | | Juvenile | |
Offence	Actual Number	Male	Female	Boys	Girls
Murder	430	265	31	16	2
Attempted murder	260	193	22	10	—
Manslaughter	34	33	2	2	1
Rape	1,079	634	3	76	2
Other sexual offences	9,946	3,134	28	344	22
Wounding	1,641	598	100	203	47
Assaults (not indecent)	77,338	24,031	1,545	1,259	168
Robbery	11,630	3,399	206	774	64
Breaking and entering	177,712	19,872	545	13,855	505
Theft—Motor vehicle	62,805	8,381	194	5,251	127
Theft over $50	150,010	11,498	1,315	3,973	373
Theft $50 and under	278,765	24,273	8,414	11,982	2,788
Have stolen goods	11,956	6,755	497	1,635	158
Frauds	67,271	13,952	2,197	488	131
Prostitution	1,887	452	1,427	1	13
Gaming and betting	1,838	2,837	198	7	—
Offensive weapons	6,440	4,169	215	384	18
Other Criminal Code	246,407	50,574	4,444	6,215	1,262
Federal Statutes	36,494	19,289	1,060	674	434
Addicting opiate like drugs	1,017	486	144	15	13
Cannabis (Marihuana)	13,054	8,110	1,082	665	120
Controlled drugs	1,007	322	39	11	2
L.S.D.	3,711	1,955	254	211	33
Provincial Statutes	335,788	219,954	15,501	4,787	2,387
Municipal By-laws	73,086	38,268	5,391	1,341	134

Source: Statistics Canada

> (a) Why is the number of people charged smaller than the number of offences?
> (b) Discuss why fewer women than men and fewer girls than boys are charged.
> (c) Discuss the reason for the frequency of crime in each category.
> (d) Check with your police department to see if statistics are available for your locality.

Secton 191(1):
Every one who obtains or attempts to obtain anything from any person by playing a game in a vehicle, aircraft or vessel used as a public conveyance for passengers is guilty of an indictable offence and is liable to imprisonment for two years.

In recent times, with the expansion of criminal law to cover new fields and to deal more adequately with matters of proof and enforcement in some of the more traditional areas of the criminal law, resort has been had to statutory changes. More frequently nowadays, a criminal liability is imposed regardless of the intention of the offender. This is particularly so in laws dealing with weights, measures, purity of food, etc.

C-2
One of the accused company's weighing clerks mistakenly filled a bag marked ten pounds with about nine pounds of sugar. The bag was sold and subsequently the company was prosecuted under the Weights and Measures Act. The Magistrate who tried the case acquitted the accused company. The Manitoba Court of Appeal reversed the Magistrate's decision and held that the statute simply prohibited selling short weight and intention was not an essential ingredient in the offence.
(a) Why was intention not considered to be an essential element in this case?
(b) Do you agree that some forms of conduct such as impaired driving should be classified as criminal regardless of intent? Why or why not?
(c) What other types of conduct could be classified in the same way?

In other areas where problems of proof have become difficult, parliament has altered the onus of proof. For example, Section 309(1):

Every one who, without lawful excuse, *the proof of which lies on him,* has in his possession any instrument suitable for housebreaking, vault-breaking or safe-breaking, under circumstances that give rise to a reasonable inference that the instrument has

been used or is or was intended to be used for housebreaking, vault-breaking or safe-breaking, is guilty of an indictable offence and is liable to imprisonment for fourteen years.

DISCUSSION

1.   In Canada the authority over criminal law is assigned to the federal government. In other federal unions, for example the United States, the authority over criminal law is vested in the component States. Discuss the advantages and disadvantages of either system.

2.   "The rights of the best of men are secure only as the rights of the vilest and most abhorrent are protected."
(Mr. Justice Pound; *People v. Gitlow,* (1922) 136 M.E. 317).
"We have long since passed the period when it is possible to punish an innocent man; we are now struggling with the problem of whether it is any longer possible to punish the guilty."
(Mr. Justice Freeman, *Roper v. Territory of New Mexico,* (1893) 33 Pacific 1014).
Compare these two statements. Do you agree with either? Why or why not?

3.   "Not the least significant test of the quality of a civilization is its treatment of those charged with crime."
(Mr. Justice Frankfurter, *Irwin v. Dowd,* (1961) 3 66 U.S. 717).
Discuss.

4.   In recent years it has been suggested that the criminal law has been relied on too heavily to control conduct in certain areas, e.g., drugs, alcohol, sex. Do you agree or not? Why? Are there other means of restraining conduct that may be considered dangerous? Discuss.

II
SPECIFIC OFFENCES

PART ONE
INTRODUCTION

In this chapter there are set out a number of specific offences for study and discussion. The offences set out have been selected somewhat arbitrarily and fall far short of being a complete list. The Criminal Code and other federal legislation create several hundred criminal offences ranging from piracy to price fixing, from giving the false alarm of a fire to dismissal of an employee because of trade union membership.

Different conditions and different times have led parliament to create many offences. Prosecution for some offences under the Criminal Code is very rare (e.g., piracy, treason) but it is obviously necessary to continue the offences.

The offences dealt with in this chapter are grouped under six categories. Some entire areas are not covered at all and even within the categories dealt with the list of offences is not complete. The collection of specific offences which follows consists largely of the offences which are committed frequently or those which attract great notoriety and are reported widely in the press. As a result of these two factors, the offences which follow are offences with which the student may have some general familiarity.

It is hoped that an analysis of the following offences will give the student an appreciation of the general nature of the criminal law and that this general understanding will apply to other offences which are not dealt with here specifically.

In consideration of each offence, we begin by reproducing the appropriate section of the Criminal Code or other statute. The section and its number are taken from the Criminal Code unless otherwise stated. Each section defines one or more specific offences.

It is a fundamental principle of our law that a person must be charged with a specific crime and not a general allegation of wrongdoing. Before a person may be convicted he must be proven guilty of the specific crime with which he is charged. The fact that the evidence discloses morally reprehensible conduct or criminal conduct different from the charge cannot justify a conviction. Example:

Harris is charged with the murder of Brown. In the course of the trial it appears that Harris traffics in narcotics, cheats on his income tax, beats his wife, and is a thoroughly detestable person. Unless the specific charge of murder is proven, he is entitled to be acquitted. If he is to be punished for any other conduct, he must be specifically charged and convicted with another offence.

There is, however, an exception to this general rule. An accused may be convicted of an offence other than the one with which he is charged if it is an included offence. An included offence is one that is part of the offence charged and is usually a lesser offence. Example:

> Manslaughter is an included offence in a charge of murder. Thus a person charged with murder may be acquitted of murder and convicted of manslaughter.
>
> Common assault is an included offence in a charge of assault causing bodily harm. Thus a person charged with assault causing bodily harm may be acquitted of that offence and convicted of common assault.

The specific section should be studied carefully. It will define a crime by describing the prohibited act and, in most cases, the prohibited state of mind which must accompany the act. The definition in many cases may appear complex and cumbersome, but experience has shown that criminal conduct must be defined with as much precision as possible. The prohibited act and its component parts, as well as the prohibited state of mind, are referred to as the elements of the offence. Each element must be present and proved before there can be a conviction. Therefore, examine each section with care to determine the elements of each offence. The text and case material which follow each section are intended to help this process.

The sections of the Criminal Code and other statutes will characterize a certain crime as an "indictable offence" or an "offence punishable on summary conviction". These terms refer to the procedure to be followed in the prosecution of an accused person. In most cases, the section will prescribe only one of the procedures. However, some sections in the Criminal Code provide that an offender is liable on indictment to one penalty and on summary conviction to a lesser penalty. In these instances, it is within the discretion of the Crown Attorney to choose which procedure he intends to follow. Even though the offences are the same, one may be less serious than another and lead the prosecution to proceed by way of summary conviction, where as in a very serious case, the prosecution may proceed by way of indictment (see chapter 5). Example:

> Dangerous driving may be proceeded with by indictment, in which case the maximum penalty is two years, or by way of summary conviction, in which case the maximum penalty is six months. In most cases the pro-

cedure is by way of summary conviction. In a flagrant and unusually serious case, the prosecution may elect to proceed by way of indictment.

Punishment

In addition to defining the crime, the section will frequently prescribe the punishment by stating that the offender is liable to imprisonment for a certain period or a fine of a stated amount. This means that the person convicted is liable to a *maximum* of the stated penalty. In these cases, the judge determines the appropriate penalty within the maximum. In rare cases, a minimum and maximum are provided. For example, a person convicted of importing a narcotic into Canada is liable to a minimum of seven years and a maximum of life imprisonment. Also, in rare instances the Criminal Code prescribes the exact penalty. For example:

> **218. (1)   Every one who commits murder punishable by death is guilty of an indictable offence and shall be sentenced to death.**

In most instances, the appropriate section will make a specific reference to penalty in one of the ways described above. In some cases, however, the section will make no reference to penalty but simply state that the offence is an indictable offence or an offence punishable on summary conviction. The Criminal Code provides that in the absence of a specific provision, summary conviction offences are punishable by a maximum of six months' imprisonment or a fine of $500, or both, and indictable offences are punishable by a maximum of five years' imprisonment.

PART TWO
OFFENCES AGAINST THE PERSON

One of the basic functions of the criminal law is to protect people against personal violence. All of us, of course, are anxious to be protected from all manner of crimes, but in the order of priorities we first need to be protected from being beaten, injured, or killed. The range of violence that the criminal law must suppress extends from the ultimate act of violence, i.e., murder, to relatively trivial assaults.

Murder

> **212.   Culpable homicide is murder**
> **(a) where the person who causes the death of a human being**
> **(i) means to cause his death, or**

> **(ii) means to cause him bodily harm that he knows is likely to cause his death, and is reckless whether death ensues or not;**
> **(b) where a person, meaning to cause death to a human being or meaning to cause him bodily harm that he knows is likely to cause his death, and being reckless whether death ensues or not, by accident or mistake causes death to another human being, notwithstanding that he does not mean to cause death or bodily harm to that human being; or**
> **(c) where a person, for an unlawful object, does anything that he knows or ought to know is likely to cause death, and thereby causes death to a human being, notwithstanding that he desires to effect his object without causing death or bodily harm to any human being.**

The criminal law classifies homicides (causing death) as either culpable or not culpable. A homicide that is not culpable is one that is caused by pure accident or in the course of self-defence, or one that is justified (e.g., a soldier or a policeman killing in the line of duty). Culpable homicide includes not only murder but also other offences which are dealt with in this book under the headings "Voluntary Manslaughter" and "Involuntary Manslaughter."

The most culpable form of homicide is, of course, murder. The common law defined murder as homicide with malice aforethought. The malice could be found in the intention of the killer or in the circumstances under which the killing took place, e.g., if a killing took place in the course of committing a crime, the malice would be implied by law. The Criminal Code now defines murder and the basic definition is contained in section 212. Section 212(a) requires little explanation. The intent to kill or cause bodily harm is usually proved by the surrounding circumstances, although occasionally psychiatric evidence is used. A jury is entitled to infer that a person intended the ordinary consequences of his act. Example:

Fowler picks up a gun, aims at Bennett, and shoots, killing him. One may conclude that Fowler intended to kill Bennett.

Section 212(b) covers the situation where a person has the required intent covered by section 212(a) but kills someone other than the intended victim. Example:

Brown loads his rifle intending to kill White. He takes careful aim, fires, but misses White and kills Black. Despite the fact that he did not intend to kill Black, this is murder.

Subsection (c) requires a less specific intent if the person causing death had an unlawful object. Example:

Daniels has a grudge against the railway which is trying to expropriate his land. He blows up a section of track to derail a train. As a result, the train crew is killed. Daniels did not intend to kill anyone. However, he performed an act for an unlawful object and should have known that his action would likely cause death. He is therefore guilty of murder.

C-1

Workman was charged with the murder of Frank Wiley in April 1962. The evidence adduced at trial showed that Wiley was a golf pro living in Edmonton with his wife and two children. Workman, a bookkeeper for a construction company, began an adulterous relationship with Mrs. Wiley.

In February of 1961 Workman had called on a lawyer to find out if a wife who committed adultery could get any of the property of her husband. When told that that was unlikely, Workman said, "We'll just have to kill him."

In July of 1961 Mrs. Wiley sued her husband for judicial separation. Mr. Wiley defended the action and counterclaimed against Workman for damages. The lawsuit was terminated by agreement in January 1962.

In April of 1962 Workman spoke to two men about having someone "worked over" and then said that he wanted him killed but wanted it to look like an accident. No name was mentioned.

On April 19 Wiley received a call ordering a set of golf clubs for $225 and asking that they be delivered at 9 o'clock that night. The same day Workman went to a home under construction by the company he worked for and asked the men there how long they would be working that night. Wiley arrived home with the golf clubs in his car, had dinner with his wife and children, and then left to deliver the golf clubs.

A neighbour gave evidence of seeing two white cars about 9 p.m., April 19, at the home where Workman had spoken to the painters. Both Wiley and Workman drove white cars. Later the police found a large amount of blood in this house despite obvious attempts to clean up.

Between 9 and 10 that evening Workman brought a tire and rim to a service station. About 3 a.m. he returned to pick it up but took away the wrong tire and rim. The wrong tire and rim were subsequently found on Wiley's car. The tire and rim that Workman had left at the service station came from Wiley's car.

On April 20 Workman hosed out the trunk of his car and then drove into the country with another man. At a certain spot, he asked the other man to drive off and come back in about twenty minutes. No explanation was given to the other man. Workman was also overheard to say he had to get back to clean the walls.

Wiley was never seen or heard of again after April 19, and his body was never found. Workman was charged with the murder of Wiley and convicted. He appealed to the Alberta Court of Appeal on the grounds that the case against him was only circumstantial and that since no body had been found, death had never been proved. His appeal was dismissed. He appealed to the Supreme Court of Canada, and that appeal was dismissed. The Supreme Court held that it was not necessary to produce a body to prove death.

    (a) On the basis of the above facts, would you have been convinced beyond a reasonable doubt that Workman murdered Wiley, despite the fact that no body was found?

    (b) If it were necessary to find a body to prove murder, could this provide killers with an easy way to avoid prosecution?

C-2

Fisher was charged with the murder of Peggy Bennett on or about June 10, 1960, at the City of Toronto. About ten days after the killing, Fisher gave a statement in which he admitted that about 9 p.m. on June 9 he had gone to a hotel where he drank until closing time shortly after midnight. Upon leaving the hotel he met Peggy Bennett, whom he knew by sight, who asked him if he had his car. They then went to a restaurant to obtain cigarettes and sat in the car smoking. Peggy Bennett made sexual advances towards Fisher, who then drove to a service station parking area. Fisher described the route he took, the traffic lights he stopped for, etc. On arriving at the service station, Fisher took a knife that he carried in the car and stabbed Peggy Bennett approximately fifteen times, killing her. He then pushed her body out of the car and drove off.

At the trial, Fisher testified that on the evening in question he had about twenty-five glasses of beer and that he had no recollection of what took place after he left the hotel. His defence was that he was so drunk he was incapable of forming the intent to cause death [212(a)(i)] or cause bodily harm [212(a)(ii)]. The prosecution called a psychiatrist who testified that, having heard Fisher's statement, it was his opinion that anyone who was able to do the things described in the statement would have had the capacity to form the intent to murder even if he had consumed twenty-five glasses of beer. Fisher was convicted.

    (a) Why do you think the prosecution called the psychiatrist?

    (b) Without the testimony of the psychiatrist, would you have been convinced that Fisher could have formed the necessary intent to murder?

C-3

Plomp was charged with the murder of his wife at Southport, Australia. On February 24, 1961, Plomp and his wife were surfing alone and Mrs. Plomp drowned. There were no witnesses. Plomp said his wife was sucked under by a wave and that he tried to help her but failed. Mrs. Plomp's body was found and bore no marks other than a slight abrasion which could have been caused by the sand. It was shown that Mrs. Plomp was a good swimmer and that the surf was not dangerous at the time.

The evidence also showed that Plomp and his wife were not getting along well, that on a prior occasion he had used violence toward her, that he was having an affair with a Miss K whom he told that his wife was dead, and that a few days before the death he introduced Miss K to one of his children as their "new mommy". Two days after the death of his wife he made arrangements to marry Miss K, arrangements which were not carried out because of the inquest into the death of his wife; he took Miss K to live with him, lied about their relationship, and tried to persuade Miss K to lie to the police about their relationship. A jury convicted Plomp of murder.

An Australian Court of Criminal Appeals dismissed Plomp's appeal on the grounds that it was for the jury to say whether or not they were satisfied beyond a reasonable doubt whether Plomp had drowned his wife or not and that there was evidence upon which they could come to this conclusion.

(a) It is sometimes said erroneously that a person cannot be convicted on circumstantial evidence alone. What does this case show?

(b) Would you have been convinced beyond a reasonable doubt that Plomp murdered his wife? Explain.

C-4

Molleur performed an abortion upon L on February 8, 1947, in Montreal. L died as a result. Molleur was charged with murder. The Crown's case was based on section 212(c) that Molleur had an unlawful object and either knew or ought to have known that his actions were likely to cause death. Molleur was convicted. He appealed to the Quebec Court of Appeal which set aside the murder conviction and substituted conviction of manslaughter on the grounds that the evidence did not show that Molleur knew or ought to have known that death was likely. In the view of the Quebec Court of Appeal, "likely" meant "probable".

(a) How does the mental state required by section 212(c) differ from that required by 212(a) and (b)?

Murder in Commission of Offences

213.   Culpable homicide is murder where a person causes the death of a human being while committing or attempting to commit treason or an offence mentioned in section 52, piracy, escape or rescue from prison or lawful custody, resisting lawful arrest, rape, indecent assault, forcible abduction, robbery, burglary or arson, whether or not the person means to cause death to any human being and whether or not he knows that death is likely to be caused to any human being, if
(a) he means to cause bodily harm for the purpose of
(i) facilitating the commission of the offence, or
(ii) facilitating his flight after committing or attempting to commit the offence,

and the death ensues from the bodily harm;

(b) he administers a stupefying or overpowering thing for a purpose mentioned in paragraph (a), and the death ensues therefrom;

(c) he wilfully stops, by any means, the breath of a human being for a purpose mentioned in paragraph (a), and the death ensues therefrom; or

(d) he uses a weapon or has it upon his person

(i) during or at the time he commits or attempts to commit the offence, or

(ii) during or at the time of his flight after committing or attempting to commit the offence,

and the death ensues as a consequence.

(Note: Section 52 referred to above covers forms of sabotage.)

As we have seen, section 212(c) requires a less specific intention when the person causing death had an unlawful purpose. Section 213 lays down an even more stringent rule if death is caused in the commission of any one of a number of serious offences. The offences are spelled out in the section itself.

A person who causes the death of another while committing one of the offences listed in section 213 may be guilty of murder, even though he did not intend death or know that it was likely, if his conduct is covered by sub-paragraphs (a), (b), (c), or (d). It will be observed that the guilty intent required is much less than required by section 212. Subparagraph (a) requires only that an offender meant to cause bodily harm to facilitate either the offence or escape. Subparagraph (d) requires only that death be caused by the use of a weapon or having it on the person.

Murder under both sections 212 and 213 is punishable by a mandatory sentence of life imprisonment. Ten years of the sentence must be served before an offender is eligible for parole. The trial judge may increase this ten-year period up to a maximum of twenty.

C-5

Simmons had given a cheque to Beatty, the operator of a service station near Simcoe, Ontario. Simmons knew the cheque was worthless and would not be cashed and would cause trouble. With another man, he went to Beatty's home to get the cheque back. Beatty refused to return the cheque and a struggle ensued between Simmons and Beatty in which Beatty was killed. The cheque was then taken (the forceful taking of the cheque constitutes robbery). Simmons was charged with murder and convicted. His appeal to the Ontario Court of Appeal was dismissed.

(a) Explain how section 213 applies to this case.

C-6

Rowe, with another, committed a robbery in Windsor, Ontario, and then hired Jolly, a taxi driver, to drive them to London about 120 miles away. While on the way to London, Jolly became suspicious of his passengers and stopped at Chatham at a service station and attempted to call the police. However, Rowe stayed with him and he was not able to call. They stopped at another service station at London, where Jolly got to a phone and succeeded in lifting the receiver and asking for the police. Rowe, however, overheard Jolly and then took out a revolver and ordered everyone to the rear of the service station saying, "This is a stickup." Rowe ordered Jolly not to go with the others. Jolly then ran through a doorway, slamming a wooden door behind him. At this point Rowe's gun fired and the bullet passed through the doorway killing Galbraith, whose presence was unknown to Rowe. Rowe testified that he had slipped on the greasy floor, causing his gun to fire, and that he had no intention of killing anyone. Rowe was convicted of murder and appealed to the Ontario Court of Appeal and subsequently to the Supreme Court of Canada. Both appeals were dismissed.

> (a) See Section 213(d). Even if Rowe's story was accepted, would it have made any difference to the verdict? Why?

Murder Punishable by Death

> **214. (1) Murder is punishable by death or is punishable by imprisonment for life.**
>
> **(2) Murder is punishable by death, in respect of any person, where such person by his own act caused or assisted in causing the death of**
>> **(a) a police officer, police constable, sheriff, deputy sheriff, sheriff's officer or other person employed for the preservation and maintenance of the public peace, acting in the course of his duties, or**
>> **(b) a warden, deputy warden, instructor, keeper, gaoler, guard or other officer or permanent employee of a prison, acting in the course of his duties,**
>
> **or counselled or procured another person to do any act causing or assisting in causing the death.**
>
> **(3) All murder other than murder punishable by death is punishable by imprisonment for life.**

In 1967 the Criminal Code was amended by what now appears as section 214. The effect of this section was to abolish capital punishment for murder except for the killing of a police officer, prison guard, etc., in the course of his or her duty. The section was placed in the Criminal Code on a trial basis for five years and, after considerable debate, was renewed for a further five years.

Voluntary Manslaughter

215. **(1) Culpable homicide that otherwise would be murder may be reduced to manslaughter if the person who committed it did so in the heat of passion caused by sudden provocation.**

(2) A wrongful act or insult that is of such a nature as to be sufficient to deprive an ordinary person of the power of self-control is provocation for the purposes of this section if the accused acted upon it on the sudden and before there was time for his passion to cool.

(3) For the purposes of this section the questions

(a) whether a particular wrongful act or insult amounted to provocation, and

(b) whether the accused was deprived of the power of self-control by the provocation that he alleges he received,

are questions of fact, but no one shall be deemed to have given provocation to another by doing anything that he had a legal right to do, or by doing anything that the accused incited him to do in order to provide the accused with an excuse for causing death or bodily harm to any human being.

Voluntary manslaughter describes that type of killing which would ordinarily be murder (under section 212) but which is reduced to manslaughter because the offender is deprived of his self-control.

The loss of self-control is described in section 215 as "in the heat of passion caused by sudden provocation".

Before an offender can be said to have acted in the heat of passion caused by sudden provocation, three conditions must exist:

(a) there must be provocation—a wrongful act or insult will amount to provocation but nothing that the victim has a legal right to do or was incited to do by the offender just to give the offender an excuse will be provocation. For example,

Samson works as a projectionist in a theatre and gets home about 2 a.m. and sleeps late. Barton, his next door neighbour, rises early. Samson's bedroom window adjoins Barton's driveway. One cold winter morning Barton starts his car and decides to warm up the motor before moving the car. He runs it for about five minutes. Barton has done this sort of thing before, to Samson's annoyance. On this morning Samson becomes furious, takes a shotgun from a closet, and shoots Barton and kills him. Samson is guilty of murder; Barton had a legal right to run his engine.

(b) the wrongful act or insult must be such that it would deprive an *ordinary* man of his self-control. An offender may, because of his nature or the consumption of drugs or alcohol, lose control because of some insult or wrongful act that would not cause an ordinary man to lose self-control. Such a loss of control is not a defence which would reduce murder to manslaughter. For example,

Arthurs, who has a terrible temper, is raking his leaves in his backyard. Robinson, his next door neighbour, is watering the lawn and playfully turns the hose on Arthurs. Arthurs becomes enraged, shouting, "I'll kill you, you lunatic", rushes at Robinson and beats him to death with the rake. Arthurs would be convicted of murder because the wrongful act (turning the hose) is not sufficient to deprive an ordinary man of self-control.

(c) the offender must actually lose self-control and must act suddenly before his passions have a chance to cool. (In deciding whether or not the offender actually lost self-control, his irascible nature or drinking or taking of drugs can be taken into account.) For example,

Jorgenson arrives home one evening to find his wife and Caldwell, his business partner, kissing in the kitchen. They explain that they are simply rehearsing their parts in an amateur theatrical production to be put on by the local PTA. Jorgenson doesn't believe a word of what he is told, but masks his feelings. Two days later he kills Caldwell. Jorgenson will be convicted of murder because he did not "act on the sudden before his passions cooled".

If a reasonable doubt exists about any of the foregoing issues, they should be resolved in favour of the accused. The maximum penalty for manslaughter is life imprisonment but shorter terms are common, depending on the facts of the case.

C-7

Taylor, his wife, and Harry Holmes had been drinking on the afternoon of November 29, 1946, and had then gone to the Taylor home near Sarnia, Ontario. More drinking took place and Taylor fell asleep. When Taylor awoke he found himself alone and was irritated, because he had warned his wife against being alone with Harry Holmes. Within a few minutes his wife entered the home and Taylor said, "You have been out with Harry Holmes." She replied, "So what? Harry Holmes is all right" and slapped him across the face. Taylor then beat his wife to death.

The trial judge told the jury that they might consider the slap as provocation, but not the words. Taylor was convicted of murder. The case was appealed to the Ontario Court of Appeal and then to the Supreme Court of Canada. The Supreme Court of Canada set aside the verdict of murder and sent the case back for a new trial, holding that under the circumstances the words could be considered as an insult and should have been considered by the jury along with the slap.

> (a) If you were a juror at the new trial, would you convict on murder or manslaughter? Why?

C-8

Galgay lived with Mary Youden, but in 1968 was sent to jail for three months. On his release he resumed living with her. In 1969, Galgay was convicted of breaking and entering and was sent to jail for twelve months. While he was serving this term he was visited by Mary Youden on December 9. She told him that she had met K, was going out with him, and wanted nothing more to do with Galgay. On December 11 Galgay escaped from the reformatory and went to Toronto where he stayed with Mary Youden. On December 13 Mary Youden left to go to the store but did not return. Galgay went to look for her and found her at the home of K. At this time Mary Youden told Galgay she had called the police and told them where he was. Galgay then asked Mary Youden to go with him to her place so that he could get his belongings. She agreed. As they walked, he asked her why she had phoned the police. She replied she didn't know. She then said she was going to live with K and said to Galgay, "You are not going to be any good; you are drinking all the time; you are stealing." Galgay then struck her, knocking her to the ground and killing her.

Galgay was charged with murder. His defence was that he was guilty only of manslaughter on the grounds of provocation. The trial judge told the jury that since Mary Youden had a right to leave him if she chose, her statement that she was going to leave could not be considered as provocation. Galgay was convicted of murder and appealed to the Ontario Court of Appeal which directed a new trial. The Appeal Court held that while Mary Youden's statement that she was going to leave could not amount to provocation, the rest of what she said could be provocation as an insult, and that this should have been explained to the jury.

> (a) In your opinion, would the subsequent remarks, "You are not going to be any good, etc." be sufficient provocation to reduce the killing to manslaughter? Discuss.

Involuntary Manslaughter

205.   (5) A person commits culpable homicide when he causes the death of a human being,
   (a) by means of an unlawful act,
   (b) by criminal negligence,
   (c) by causing that human being, by threats or fear of violence or by deception, to do anything that causes his death, or
   (d) wilfully frightening that human being, in the case of a child or sick person.
217.   Culpable homicide that is not murder or infanticide is manslaughter.

The crime of involuntary manslaughter is something of a catch-all. There are many cases where a person causes the death of another that do not amount to murder. Yet if the homicide is unlawful (i.e., neither accidental nor justified), there is still guilt attached to the homicide. Example:

> Bannister, a jealous husband, while waiting for his wife to come home from a movie, begins drinking and brooding about the fact that she is late. When she returns, they argue about the fact that she is late. Bannister loses his temper and slaps his wife across the side of the head, causing her to fall against the fireplace. She dies of a head injury.

For Bannister to be guilty of murder, a jury would have to be satisfied beyond a reasonable doubt that (a) he meant to cause death or (b) he meant to cause bodily harm which he knew was likely to cause death and was reckless as to whether death ensued or not. It is not likely that Bannister would be guilty of murder but, as will be shown, he would be guilty of manslaughter. Section 205 of the Criminal Code defines "culpable homicide". Section 217 says that culpable homicide which is not either (a) murder or (b) infanticide (the killing of a newly born child by a mother before she has recovered from the effects of childbirth and while her mind is disturbed) is manslaughter.

"Involuntary manslaughter" then is defined by looking at the wide definition of "culpable homicide" in section 205. It will be recalled that "murder" is defined as a type of culpable homicide but in more specific terms. Everything that remains after deducting murder and infanticide will constitute manslaughter.

Section 205 sets out four classes of killing which are culpable:

(a) by means of an unlawful act. This is the widest class. Any unlawful act which causes death will be covered under this subsection. For example, striking someone, placing a drug in the food and drink of another, cutting a brake cable, are all unlawful acts and if death is caused will amount to manslaughter. An unlawful act, however, does not include acts that are simply breaches of merely regulatory statutes, provincial laws, and municipal by-laws.

(b) by criminal negligence. The Criminal Code provides that everyone is criminally negligent who

    (i)   in doing anything or

    (ii) in omitting to do anything that it is his duty to do shows a wanton or reckless disregard for the lives and safety of other persons.

Criminal negligence would have been covered under (a) as an unlawful act, but subsection 205(b) appears in the Criminal Code to remove any doubt.

Paragraphs (c) and (d) in section 205 are two more examples of causing death by acts that would fall under the definition "by means of an unlawful act" but which have been added for greater certainty.

The maximum penalty for involuntary manslaughter is life imprisonment, but relatively modest sentences are common and depend on the circumstances.

C-9

D'Angelo sold alcohol for beverage purposes to two persons. D'Angelo swore that he believed the alcohol to be grain alcohol. It turned out that it was wood alcohol, which is poisonous, and the purchasers died. At the time, a statute existed in Ontario which prohibited the sale of any type of alcohol. D'Angelo was charged with murder.

The trial judge instructed the jury that selling alcohol was an "unlawful act" and if the victims died as a result of drinking it, D'Angelo would be guilty of manslaughter. D'Angelo was convicted. He appealed to the Ontario Court of Appeal, which directed a new trial. The Court of Appeal held that mere breach of provincial legislation was not "unlawful" as required as an element of manslaughter. The Court of Appeal held, however, that D'Angelo could be convicted if the jury was satisfied that he was criminally negligent in selling the wrong kind of alcohol.

> (a) If D'Angelo had caused death by selling a narcotic drug, would the result be different? Explain.

C-10

Larkin lived with a woman and was accustomed to giving her his pay cheque. On September 28, 1941, he went looking for her to ask for some of the money. He found her drinking with two other women and a man named Neilsen. Larkin was upset, but went away. After brooding about the matter he returned with a razor in his pocket. Larkin testified that he took out the razor, brandished it at Neilsen and at this point his woman friend, who was groggy with drink, swayed against him, cutting her throat on the razor. There was other evidence which contradicted Larkin.

Larkin, charged with murder, was convicted of manslaughter. He appealed to the English Court of Appeal, who dismissed his appeal. It was held that even on his own story he was guilty of an assault on Neilsen (an unlawful act) which caused the death of the woman.

> (a) What change in the above facts would have led to the acquittal of Larkin?

C-11

Lamb purchased a Smith and Wesson revolver. The gun had a five-chambered cylinder which rotated when the trigger was pulled. Lamb, as a joke, pointed the gun at his best friend. The gun at that time had two bullets in the chambers but none in the chamber opposite the barrel. Lamb then pulled the trigger. The gun fired and killed his friend. The reason the gun fired was that the pulling of the trigger caused the cylinder to rotate, placing a bullet opposite the barrel when it was struck by the firing pin.

Lamb was charged with manslaughter. The prosecution argued that Lamb's conduct amounted to criminal negligence. Lamb was convicted and appealed to the English Court of Appeal. Lamb's appeal was allowed because the trial judge did not adequately explain to the jury the defence of accident. Expert evidence had been called at the trial to show that such a mistake was natural for one unfamiliar with the mechanism.

    (a) What is criminal negligence?
    (b) In your opinion, did Lamb's conduct amount to criminal negligence?

Common Assault

> **245. (1) Every one who commits a common assault is guilty of an offence punishable on summary conviction.**
>
> **(2) Every one who unlawfully causes bodily harm to any person or committs an assault that causes bodily harm to any person is guilty of an indictable offence and is liable to imprisonment for five years.**
>
> **244. A person commits an assault when, without the consent of another person or with consent, where it is obtained by fraud,**
>
> **(a) he applies force intentionally to the person of the other, directly or indirectly, or**
>
> **(b) he attempts or threatens, by an act or gesture, to apply force to the person of the other, if he has or causes the other to believe upon reasonable grounds that he has present ability to effect his purpose.**

An assault is an interference with a person and is a type of violence. Assault as defined in section 244 is simply the intentional application of force to another without consent. Section 244(b) provides that a threat accompanied by an act or gesture (e.g., shaking a fist) may be an assault if there is good reason to believe that the person is able to carry out his purpose. Section 245(1) deals with common assault, which is simply an assault as defined by section 244. Section 245(2) deals with a more serious offence, an assault which causes bodily harm. Bodily harm includes any actual harm—any cut, bruise, etc., is actually bodily harm.

There are more serious types of assault, e.g., causing bodily harm with intent to wound [section 228] (which are not dealt with here).

C-12

Fowler, while driving his car, was followed by a car driven by Gaiter, Cuccio, and Judge. Fowler pulled into a place near where he lived and the other car stopped; the three occupants got out and walked towards the Fowler car. Fowler locked the doors of his car but left the window down slightly.

Gaiter made a motion as if to show that he had a weapon and said to Fowler that he would burn him. Judge said, "Yes, he would do it." Then either Gaiter or Cuccio tried the door and Cuccio tore off the aerial. There was no physical violence to Fowler. All three were charged and convicted of common assault. An appeal was taken to the Ontario Court of Appeal. The Appeal Court referred to the definition of "assault" in the Criminal Code and were of the opinion that it covered the conduct of Gaiter and Cuccio. Despite the fact that Judge did nothing but speak, he was a party to the common purpose (see Parties to an Offence). The appeal was dismissed.

> (a) Explain why the conduct of Gaiter and Cuccio was an assault.

C-13

MacTavish and Mitchell were high school students in New Brunswick. Mitchell saw MacTavish throwing snowballs at Mitchell's brother's car and told him to stop. MacTavish took offence because this took place in the presence of his girl friend. Later in the day MacTavish challenged Mitchell to a fight. The next day Mitchell agreed to a fist fight outside the school building.

They met in the presence of a large number of students. Each took off his jacket and threw some punches. MacTavish then got a headlock on Mitchell and forced him to the ground and pulled his sweater over his head. While Mitchell was down with his sweater over his head MacTavish kicked him several times in the head until he was stopped. Mitchell suffered a broken nose, probable fracture of the sinus, and other injuries. Mitchell was hospitalized for four days. MacTavish was charged with common assault and convicted by the magistrate on the grounds that Mitchell had only consented to a schoolboy fight, not to kicking involving bodily injury as a probable consequence. MacTavish appealed to the New Brunswick Court of Appeal. The appeal was dismissed.

> (a) Do you agree with this decision? Discuss.

C-14

In September of 1969, the St. Louis Blues and the Boston Bruins played an exhibition game in Ottawa. During the first period, Green pushed Maki in the mouth with a glove and a delayed penalty was signalled. There was contradictory evidence as to whether Maki speared Green. Then both players came together, sticks swinging. Green swung at Maki with his stick, striking him on the neck and shoulder. Maki then swung at Green, his stick glancing off Green's stick and striking Green on the side of the head, causing a very serious head injury. Maki was charged with assault causing bodily harm. The provincial judge held that those who agree to play hockey agree to accept the risks and hazards of the sport and in most cases this agreement would be a sufficient defence to a charge of assault. However, no hockey player is presumed to accept a malicious, unprovoked, or overly violent attack. The Provincial Judge went on to acquit Maki on the grounds that he was not satisfied beyond a reasonable doubt that Maki was not acting in self-defence.

> (a) Would the degree of violence that a participant agrees to accept vary with the sport in which he participates? Explain.

C-15

Starrat, a police officer in plain clothes, attempted to arrest V for certain liquor offences. In attempting to retain certain evidence, i.e., a bottle of wine, Starrat swung a pair of handcuffs which hit V in the mouth and knocked out some teeth. Starrat was charged with assault causing bodily harm. The Provincial Judge found that Starrat did not intend to hit V with the handcuffs but was careless in swinging them. The Provincial Judge convicted Starrat. The Ontario Court of Appeal reversed the conviction.

> (a) Why was Starrat's action not an assault?

Assault with Intent

> **246.   (1) Every one who assaults a person with intent to commit an indictable offence is guilty of an indictable offence and is liable to imprisonment for five years.**
>
> **(2) Every one who**
>   **(a) assaults a public officer or peace officer engaged in the execution of his duty, or a person acting in aid of such an officer;**
>   **(b) assaults a person with intent to resist or prevent the lawful arrest or detention of himself or another person; or**
>   **(c) assaults a person**
>   **(i) who is engaged in the lawful execution of a process against lands or goods or in making a lawful distress or seizure, or**
>   **(ii) with intent to rescue anything taken under a lawful process, distress or seizure,**
> **is guilty of**
>   **(d) an indictable offence and is liable to imprisonment for five years, or**
>   **(e) an offence punishable on summary conviction.**

The law makes common assault a crime and makes assault which causes bodily harm a more serious crime. Similarly, the criminal law has classified certain other assaults (regardless of whether or not they cause bodily harm) as more serious. Generally the latter are assaults for the purpose of committing some other indictable offence or assaults on a person engaged in law enforcement.

C-16

Fagan was driving a car in London, England. A police officer gave him directions as to where to park. At first Fagan parked his car too far from the curb and the officer then asked him to park closer. Fagan drove forward toward the officer and stopped with his front tire on the officer's foot. "Get off my foot," said the officer. "F—— you, you can wait," said Fagan. Fagan turned off the ignition, the officer again told him to move his car from his foot and Fagan then said, "Okay, man, okay" and slowly turned on the ignition and backed off the officer's foot.

Fagan was charged with assaulting a police officer in the execution of his duty. At trial it could not be shown whether or not the initial driving on to the officer's foot was deliberate or accidental. The trial court, however, was satisfied that Fagan had deliberately allowed the car to remain on the officer's foot unnecessarily. Fagan was convicted.

Fagan appealed. The English Court of Appeal agreed that negligently driving a car on to the officer's foot was not assault nor is the failure to do something an assault. The Appeal Court found, however, that the car's being on the officer's foot was a continuing act and that Fagan deliberately kept the car in that position by turning off the ignition, and that this constituted an assault. The appeal was dismissed.

(a) In what duty was the officer engaged?
(b) Why was driving on to the officer's foot not an assault?

C-17

Lascelles had loaned his car to another man who was arrested by the police on a charge of dangerous driving and taken into custody. The car was also detained by the police. Later Mr. Lascelles came along and asked to take two cartons of milk from the car. He was given permission to do this and entered the car. He took the two cartons of milk and also an envelope from the glove compartment which contained a hydro bill. The officer objected to his taking the envelope and arrested Lascelles, who in turn tried to kick the officer. Lascelles was charged with assaulting a police officer in the execution of his duty.

He was convicted by the Provincial Judge. Lascelles appealed to the Ontario Court of Appeal who acquitted him on the grounds that the police officer had no right to arrest him and was therefore not in the execution of his duty.

(a) What two elements need be proved to constitute this offence?
(b) Was Lascelles guilty of some other offence?

Abortion

251.   (1) Every one who, with intent to procure the miscarriage of a female person, whether or not she is pregnant, uses any means for the purpose of carrying out his intention is guilty of an indictable offence and is liable to imprisonment for life.

(2) Every female person who, being pregnant, with intent to procure her own miscarriage, uses any means or permits any means to be used for the purpose of carrying out her intention is guilty of an indictable offence and is liable to imprisonment for two years.

(3) In this section, "means" includes

(a) the administration of a drug or other noxious thing,

(b) the use of an instrument, and

(c) manipulation of any kind.

(4) Subsections (1) and (2) do not apply to

(a) a qualified medical practitioner, other than a member of a therapeutic abortion committee for any hospital, who in good faith uses in an accredited or approved hospital any means for the purpose of carrying out his intention to procure the miscarriage of a female person, or

(b) a female person who, being pregnant, permits a qualified medical practitioner to use in an accredited or approved hospital any means described in paragraph (a) for the purpose of carrying out her intention to procure her own miscarriage,

if, before the use of those means, the therapeutic abortion committee for that accredited or approved hospital, by a majority of the members of the committee and at a meeting of the committee at which the case of such female person has been reviewed,

(c) has by certificate in writing stated that in its opinion the continuation of the pregnancy of such female person would or would be likely to endanger her life or health, and

(d) has caused a copy of such certificate to be given to the qualified medical practitioner.

In recent years abortion has been the subject of much argument and discussion. Some argue that a woman should have the right to terminate her pregnancy if she wishes; others argue that an unborn child has the right to live and should not be destroyed because the mother simply wishes to terminate her pregnancy. The present law prohibits "the use of any means with intent to procure a miscarriage". It is an offence for a person to administer such treatment and also for a person to submit to such treatment. It is not material that the woman is not pregnant; presumably those involved would think that she was, in order to have an intention to procure a miscarriage. Even if it is shown that they were mistaken, this will not be a defence. As long as the necessary intention is present, it is also immaterial that the use of means failed to bring about a miscarriage.

Subsection (4) provides that lawful abortions may be performed by a qualified medical practitioner with the approval of an abortion committee at an accredited hospital, if continued pregnancy will endanger the life and health of the mother.

C-18

Miss V became pregnant and through others was put in touch with Lariviere. V made several visits to Lariviere, who used instruments for the stated purpose of enlarging the womb. On about the fourth visit the issue of money arose and payment was arranged. After the fifth visit V became very ill with pains in the abdomen and vaginal bleeding. She entered the hospital, where it was ascertained that a miscarriage had taken place. Lariviere was charged under section 251(1), i.e., using means with intent to procure a miscarriage. At the trial there was evidence that V had taken some pills during her pregnancy and it was argued that they, not Lariviere's treatment, caused the miscarriage. Lariviere denied using any instruments on V and said she was simply sheltering the girl during difficult times. The jury convicted Lariviere, who appealed to the Quebec Court of Appeal. One of the grounds raised on appeal was that it had not been proved that Lariviere had caused the miscarriage. The Quebec Court of Appeal said the offence was committed when one used means with intent to procure a miscarriage and it was not necessary that the miscarriage be actually caused.

> (a) Read section 251. Do you agree with the Quebec Court of Appeal?

CASES FOR DISCUSSION

1.   Slade returns home from a business trip a day earlier than expected and finds his wife in the arms of Marshall, his chief business rival. Slade, who some say has ice water in his veins, says, "What a splendid opportunity to get rid of both of you. I'll get a short sentence for manslaughter and an early parole." He then shoots both, killing them. Slade's remarks were overheard by a repairman who was fixing the furnace and was able to hear through the hot air ducts. Slade is charged with murder.

> (a) Will he be convicted of murder or manslaughter? Discuss.

2.   Foster, an employee of the Fabulous Furniture Factory, is fired. Foster feels that he was not treated fairly and decides to seek revenge by setting fire to the factory (arson). Late one night he gains access to the factory property and sets fire in the area of the plant where the waste material is kept. As he is about to leave, he encounters the night watchman. The watchman shouts, "Stop!" Foster strikes the watchman with his fist and runs. The watchman, an elderly man, falls to the cement floor, striking his head, and is killed. The fire department arrive quickly, extinguish the fire, and find the watchman. Foster is arrested and gives a statement in which he admits the above facts and states that while he struck the watchman he did not intend to kill him.

> (a) Is he guilty? Give reasons for your answer.

3.   Snodgrass is seated at a banquet table directly opposite McSwine. McSwine consumes the last ounce of soup from his bowl by raising it to his lips, drinks tea from his saucer, and eats peas from his knife. Finally, Snodgrass, unable to control himself any longer, leans forward towards McSwine and says in a low voice, "If there were no ladies present I would stuff these olives up your nose." McSwine, surprised and hurt by the words, stands up abruptly, tipping a hot fudge sundae into Snodgrass's lap. Each charges the other with assault.

   (a) Is either guilty? Explain.

4.   For years Gallagher has been irritated by the noise of high-powered cars tearing up and down his street in the middle of the night. One night when the noise had been particularly bad, he could stand it no longer. Taking his shotgun from the closet, he ran to the front porch and fired at a passing car. The shotgun blast struck the right front tire of the car, causing a blow-out. The vehicle went out of control, striking a tree and killing the driver.

   (a) Is Gallagher guilty of (i) murder, (ii) manslaughter, or (iii) not guilty of either one? Explain.

5.   Connolly and three friends decide to play a form of Russian roulette. Connolly produces a revolver and places one cartridge in the cylinder and then spins the cylinder. He points the gun at Nolan and pulls the trigger, producing a click as the hammer strikes an empty cylinder. Once again the cylinder is spun and Connolly points the gun at Boyd and pulls the trigger. The gun fires, killing Boyd.

(a) Is Connolly guilty of (i) murder or (ii) manslaughter? Discuss.

PART THREE
OFFENCES AGAINST PROPERTY RIGHTS

One of the objects of the criminal law is the protection of our property rights against interference or seizure by others. Earlier in the history of the criminal law, the protection of property appeared to be one of its primary functions. In the not too distant past, many forms of theft were punishable by death. It is said that the criminal law was overly concerned with the protection of property and served the interests of the rich and powerful. However, in more primitive times, many forms of property (horses, livestock, weapons) were of more critical importance than any property is today and perhaps warranted greater protection. Many modern writers point to the very large maximum penalties still contained in the Criminal Code and argue that the criminal law continues to over-emphasize property rights.

The three offences that follow have always been among the most frequently committed crimes. The infliction of severe penalties in the past did nothing to lessen the number of offences then, nor has a more enlightened modern attitude been particularly successful.

Theft

> **283.   (1) Every one commits theft who fraudulently and without colour of right takes, or fraudulently and without colour of right converts to his use or to the use of another person, anything whether animate or inanimate, with intent,**
>
> > **(a) to deprive, temporarily or absolutely, the owner of it or a person who has a special property or interest in it, of the thing or of his property or interest in it,**
> >
> > **(b) to pledge it or deposit it as security,**
> >
> > **(c) to part with it under a condition with respect to its return that the person who parts with it may be unable to perform, or**
> >
> > **(d) to deal with it in such a manner in which it was at the time it was taken or converted.**
>
> **(2) A person commits theft when, with intent to steal anything, he moves it or causes it to be moved, or begins to cause it to become movable.**
>
> **(3) A taking or conversion of anything may be fraudulent notwithstanding that it is effected without secrecy or attempt at concealment.**
>
> **(4) For the purposes of this Act the question whether anything that is converted is taken for the purpose of conversion, or whether it is, at the time it is converted, in the lawful possession of the person who converts it is not material.**
>
> **294.   Except where otherwise prescribed by law, every one who commits theft is guilty of an indictable offence and is liable**
>
> > **(a) to imprisonment for ten years, where the property stolen is a testamentary instrument or where the value of what is stolen exceeds two hundred dollars, or**
> >
> > **(b) to imprisonment for two years, where the value of what is stolen does not exceed two hundred dollars.**

Two elements are required for theft:
  (a) the act of taking or converting (appropriating),
  (b) the necessary intention.

The act of taking is self-explanatory. Converting may occur when one already has possession of goods for one purpose and then converts or appropriates them to his own purposes. Example:

> Simms, a delivery boy, is given a number of gifts to distribute to customers. He keeps one for himself. He acquired possession of the gifts lawfully from his employer, but he committed theft when he converted or appropriated one of the gifts to his own use.

Section 283(2) makes the meaning of "taking" or "converting" more precise by providing that simply moving an object or beginning to move it will be sufficient to constitute the taking or converting.

The necessary mental element for theft is twofold:

(1) the taking or converting must be fraudulent and without colour of right. If the taking or converting is not fraudulent or if a person believes he has a right to an item, even though he may be wrong, he will not be guilty of theft.

(2) Further, the person who takes or converts must do so with intent to accomplish one of the purposes set out in paragraphs (a), (b), (c) or (d) of Section 283(1).

Finally, it must be added that goods must be stolen from somebody, either the owner or someone who has a lesser interest in the goods (a person who is storing the goods, a pawnbroker, etc.). Goods which are abandoned and ownerless cannot be stolen.

For the purposes of penalty, theft is divided into two classes: theft over two hundred dollars and theft under two hundred dollars. (This division was formerly fixed at fifty dollars until the recognition of the diminishing value of the dollar caused parliament to alter it.) When one is charged with theft, the charge must indicate whether the prosecution alleges theft over or under two hundred dollars.

Some special types of theft that would be difficult to fit within the old concepts have been treated separately in the Criminal Code, e.g., theft of a telecommunication service (Section 287). Other thefts are treated separately as being more serious, e.g., theft from the mails (Section 314).

C-1

On Saturday afternoon, January 18, 1964, a meter enforcing officer was making his rounds of the parking meters in Stratford, Ontario. He was driving a three-wheeled vehicle called a Servicar. He stopped to make out a parking ticket and as he did so, Wilkins, a friend of the car owner who was getting the ticket, took the Servicar intending to drive it a short distance to play a joke on the officer. Wilkins was charged with theft over fifty dollars and convicted. He appealed to the Ontario Court of Appeal, which acquitted him. The Ontario Court of Appeal was composed of three judges, two of whom were of the opinion that Wilkins should be acquitted and one of whom felt that the conviction should stand. The majority were of the opinion that the taking of the Servicar was not fraudulent; the dissenting judge was of the opinion that the taking was intended to temporarily deprive the officer of the Servicar.

(a) Do you agree with the majority or the minority? Discuss.

C-2

Hibbert was arrested on the Reddish Vale Golf Links, England, in October 1947. He had in his possession eight golf balls which he had picked up on the course that day and which had been abandoned by their original owners. He gave a false name and address, denied possession of the golf balls, and later stated that he knew he had no right to take them. The golf club was jointly owned by the members of the club. Hibbert had been warned off the course on prior occasions.

Hibbert was convicted of theft and appealed to an English Appeal Court. The Appeal Court held that Hibbert was not an honest finder and that the taking was therefore fraudulent. The Court further held that the members of the club retained ownership in the balls because they were still on their land and within their control since others were warned off.

(a) Would it make any difference if the course were a public course?
(b) Spectators at major league baseball games keep fly balls hit into the stands. Is this theft? Why or why not?

C-3

The Reverend Henry Cunlisse, a passenger on the Shrewsbury and Birmingham Railway, accidentally left a piece of luggage in one of the compartments. Pugh, an employee of the railroad, found the piece of luggage at one of the station stops, and turned it over to Pearce, the engineer. Pearce pried open the luggage with a wrench and divided the contents between himself and Pugh. Both were charged and convicted of theft.

(a) When Pugh found the luggage, what should he have done?
(b) Was it theft for Pugh to take the luggage from the compartment when he found it?
(c) When did the theft take place?

Robbery

302.   Every one commits robbery who
(a) steals, and for the purpose of extorting whatever is stolen or to prevent or overcome resistance to the stealing, uses violence or threats of violence to a person or property;
(b) steals from any person and, at the time he steals or immediately before or immediately thereafter, wounds, beats, strikes or uses any personal violence to that person;
(c) assaults any person with intent to steal from him; or
(d) steals from any person while armed with an offensive weapon or imitation thereof.
303.   Every one who commits robbery is guilty of an indictable offence and is liable to imprisonment for life.

In general terms, robbery is an aggravated form of theft involving violence or the possibility of violence to the victim. Robbery, therefore, is composed basically of two elements:
(1) theft or the intention to commit theft and
(2) violence or its possibility.
Subsection (a) sets out the basic definition, i.e., theft accompanied by violence or threats to facilitate the theft.

Subsection (b) adds an extended meaning of robbery. Thus, the definition of robbery in section 302 includes any case where theft takes place and violence is used to the victim either before, during or after the theft.

Subsection (c) provides that an assault with intent to steal is robbery whether the theft takes place or not.

Subsection (d) provides that stealing while armed whether the weapon is used or not is robbery.

C-4

Neuman invited Lieberman and three others to his apartment where some drinking took place. In the course of the evening a fight took place between Lieberman and Neuman and as a result Neuman was taken to hospital. When he returned, Neuman discovered that his wallet, containing about $100, was missing, as well as a bottle of whisky and his wristwatch. The watch was found in the possession of Lieberman, who was charged with robbery. Lieberman testified that the fight was started by Neuman and he was simply defending himself. He said that he had the watch because Neuman had asked him to fix the strap on it. The trial judge instructed the jury that they should either convict of robbery or acquit.

Lieberman was convicted and appealed to the Ontario Court of Appeal. The Appeal Court directed a new trial on the basis that there were three possible verdicts:
  (a) guilty of robbery,
  (b) guilty of theft,
  (c) not guilty.

The Appeal Court pointed out that the jury might have accepted the self-defence theory with respect to the violence even though they did not accept the explanation for the possession of the watch, in which case the offence would be simply theft.

  (a) What two elements make up the offence of robbery?
  (b) What should the trial judge tell the jury about the possible verdict on the new trial?

C-5

Ford and Armstrong were tried for robbery. The evidence showed that Ford and one Lane had been up all night playing cards and that in the course of the game Ford lost $600 to Lane. It was suggested that Lane had cheated. The next morning Ford, assisted by Armstrong, went to Lane, assaulted him, and took back most of the $600 but without touching other amounts of cash and valuables. The trial judge instructed the jury that if Ford and Armstrong were of the honest (though mistaken) belief that Ford had been cheated out of his money and that they were entitled to recover it, they should acquit Armstrong and Ford of robbery. The two were acquitted of robbery but convicted of common assault.

  (a) If Lane had not been present when Armstrong and Ford recovered the money, would the taking have amounted to theft?
  (b) Can a taking that would not constitute theft, coupled with violence, amount to robbery?

Breaking and Entering

306. (1) Every one who
(a) breaks and enters a place with intent to commit an indictable offence therein,
(b) breaks and enters a place and commits an indictable offence therein, or
(c) breaks out of a place after
(i) committing an indictable offence therein, or
(ii) entering the place with intent to commit an indictable offence therein,
is guilty of an indictable offence and is liable
(d) to imprisonment for life, if the offence is committed in relation to a dwelling-house, or
(e) to imprisonment for fourteen years, if the offence is committed in relation to a place other than a dwelling-house.
(2) For the purposes of proceedings under this section, evidence that an accused
(a) broke and entered a place is, in the absence of any evidence to the contrary, proof that he broke and entered with intent to commit an indictable offence therein; or
(b) broke out of a place is, in the absence of any evidence to the contrary, proof that he broke out after
(i) committing an indictable offence therein, or
(ii) entering with intent to commit an indictable offence therein.
282.   In this Part
"break" means
(a) to break any part, internal or external, or
(b) to open any thing that is used or intended to be used to close or to cover an internal or external opening;
308.   For the purposes of sections 306 and 307,
(a) a person enters as soon as any part of his body or any part of an instrument that he uses is within any thing that is being entered; and
(b) a person shall be deemed to have broken and entered if
(i) he obtained entrance by a threat or artifice or by collusion with a person within, or
(ii) he entered without lawful justification or excuse, the proof of which lies upon him, by a permanent or temporary opening.

At common law the offence that is now known as breaking and entering was described as burglary. The basic elements are:
(1) the breaking and entry
(2) the intent to commit some indictable offence or the actual commission of an indictable offence.

Breaking

Section 282 enlarges the ordinary meaning of "breaking". Simply opening an unlocked door would be breaking. Section 308 defines what constitutes "entering". Section 308(b)(i) provides that entrance obtained in any one of several ways will be deemed to be breaking and entry despite the fact that there has been no break-in in the ordinary sense. It is to be noted as well that Section 306(c) adds the offence of "breaking out".

Commission of an Indictable Offence or
Intent to Commit an Indictable Offence

Breaking and entering alone do not constitute the offence, although in some instances if there is damage to the property there may be a different offence. There must be an intent to commit the indictable offence or its actual commission. The most common indictable offence that is the object of the break-in is theft. However, the offence is not restricted to break-ins of that nature. The object of the break-in may be any indictable offence, e.g., rape, assault, etc. Section 306(2) provides that the fact that a person broke in is, in the absence of any evidence to the contrary, evidence that the person entered to commit an indictable offence once inside. Example:

> Burns jimmies the back window of a service station at 3 a.m., and enters. In the station building he is caught by the police. Nothing is missing. The fact that Burns broke and entered the station, in the absence of any evidence to the contrary, is evidence that he intended to commit an indictable offence in the station, for example, theft.

At one time our law contained a variety of classes of break-ins. It was considered to be more serious to break into a house than into a place of business and more serious to break and enter at night than in the daytime. Many of these distinctions have now been abolished.

Breaking and entering is considered a serious crime, not only because of the property rights involved, i.e., the building and its contents, but because of the potential danger to the occupants.

> **C-6**
> Corkum was charged that on September 20, 1968, he did unlawfully break and enter a place, to wit, the dwelling house of Shirley Wood, and commit theft contrary to the Criminal Code. The evidence showed that Corkum had gained entry by raising an unlocked and partly opened window leading into Shirley Wood's kitchen and had stolen two wheels and tires. Corkum's lawyer raised the defence that there had been no "breaking". A Nova Scotia County Court judge convicted the accused.
>
> > (a) How does the Criminal Code define "breaking"?
> > (b) What did Corkum do which constituted breaking?

C-7

On March 15, 1968, MacLeod and another went to the home of some neighbours where some drinking took place. MacLeod became involved in an argument and left the premises. Later he returned, broke a window, and entered the house seeking something further to drink from the bottle that he and the friend had brought earlier. MacLeod was charged with breaking and entering and was convicted. On appeal to the Supreme Court of Prince Edward Island, the conviction was reversed.

   (a) What are the necessary elements for the offence of breaking and entering?
   (b) Why did the Supreme Court of Prince Edward Island reverse the conviction?

C-8

In July 1970, Bargiamis offered C $1000 if he would leave open the back door of the Zumburger Restaurant at Bloor and Yonge Streets in Toronto. C, who was the assistant night manager, notified his employer and the police and then pretended to go along with the scheme. Bargiamis entered through the unlocked door and proceeded through the basement and into the restaurant, where he was arrested. He was wearing socks on his hands and was carrying a crowbar. He was charged with breaking and entering with intent to commit an indictable offence. He was convicted by the Provincial Judge and appealed to the Ontario Court of Appeal. His argument was that there was no breaking and entering since he had been let in with the consent of the assistant night manager. The Ontario Court of Appeal, relying on Section 308(b)(ii), dismissed the appeal.

   (a) What is the effect of Section 308(b)(ii)?
   (b) How does that subsection apply to this case?

CASES FOR DISCUSSION

1.   Jenkins, a farmer, noticed that sheep from a distant neighbour's farm had strayed on to his land and had mingled with his flock. Jenkins did nothing, in the hope that they would not be found. Several days later he noticed that the neighbour's sheep were beginning to stray away. He then drove them back amongst his own.

   (a) Did Jenkins commit theft?
   (b) If a theft did take place, when did it take place?

C-9

2.   Skivington went to the firm where both he and his wife worked, with a letter authorizing him to collect his wife's wages. Skivington asked for his own wages and his wife's. It was Wednesday and wages were not ordinarily due until Friday. Skivington testified that he honestly believed he was entitled to the money on Wednesday. A fracas took place which culminated in the assistant manager's giving Skivington the two pay envelopes at the point of a knife. Skivington was charged with robbery.

   (a) Is Skivington guilty of robbery? Why or why not?
   (b) Is he guilty of anything else?

3. Sherman is the captain of the football team at Keewatin High School. One night, a week before the annual game against their perennial rival, Baffin High School, Sherman leads a group of his team mates to Baffin High School where they abduct Marvin, a 600-pound polar bear, the Baffin High School mascot. The next day Marvin's absence is discovered and a large-scale search begins. The day before the game, Marvin is discovered in the Keewatin High School pool, swimming contentedly among ice cubes. You are the local RCMP officer. Officials at Baffin High School ask you to arrest Sherman and charge him with theft.

    (a) What is your answer?

4. Jurgens obtains a fireman's uniform from a used clothing store. Wearing the uniform, he calls at the home of Cassidy. Mrs. Cassidy answers the door and Jurgens tells her that he is an inspector from the fire marshal's office conducting a neighbourhood safety check. He is admitted to the house and makes a detailed inspection of it. When he departs, Mrs. Cassidy finds certain items of jewellery and $300 in cash have been stolen. Jurgens is found and charged that he "did break and enter and commit and indictable offence therein, namely theft".

    (a) Is he guilty? Why or why not?

5. Owens and Walker, who are both armed, go to the house of Dickson, who is the local manager of the Bank of Montreal. Mrs. Dickson answers the door and the two men ask to see Mr. Dickson. She lets them into the house and calls her husband. When Mr. Dickson appears, Owens and Walker produce revolvers and tell Mr. and Mrs. Dickson not to panic. Mr. Dickson is told to telephone his assistant at the bank and have him prepare a package containing $200,000 to be picked up by a "Mr. Smith". Dickson explains to his assistant that he and his wife are being held hostage. Owens then leaves the Dickson home and proceeds to the bank, where he identifies himself as Mr. Smith and picks up the package. He returns to the Dickson house, where he helps Walker bind and gag the Dicksons. Owens and Walker then flee, but are arrested a few days later.

    (a) With which of the offences dealt with in this Part can Owens and Walker be charged?

PART FOUR
SEXUAL OFFENCES

The following offences, as the title suggests, are concerned with sex. In some of the areas involved, the criminal law is concerned with the protection of the person from sexual violation, e.g., rape; other areas (e.g., obscenity) are more concerned with maintaining moral standards and, as will be seen, are more difficult to apply.

Rape

> **143.   A male person commits rape when he has sexual inter-course with a female person who is not his wife,**
>   **(a) without her consent, or**
>   **(b) with her consent if the consent**
>   **(i) is extorted by threats or fear of bodily harm,**
>   **(ii) is obtained by personating her husband, or**
>   **(iii) is obtained by false and fraudulent representations as to the nature and quality of the act.**
> **144.   Every one who commits rape is guilty of an indictable offence and is liable to imprisonment for life.**

The nature of this extremely serious offence is fairly simple. The offence has two basic elements: (a) the act of intercourse, and (b) the absence of consent (consent procured by threats of fraud is not real consent).

In some cases there may be a conflict of evidence as to whether or not intercourse took place or a dispute as to whether or not the person accused is the one who performed the act, but in most cases the contest revolves around the issue of consent: i.e., the victim says that there was intercourse against her will; the accused says that there was intercourse but with consent.

The burden of proof is on the prosecution to prove lack of consent, and lack of consent simply means "against the will of" or "without permission of" the woman. If a woman first resists but then changes her mind, she will be held to have consented.

However, a consent that is obtained by fraud is not real consent nor is consent real that is obtained by threats or genuine fear. Generally, chastity or the lack of it in the victim makes no difference with respect to the offence of rape. A prostitute can be raped—the issue is whether or not she consents. However, a court may look at the previous character of the victim in determining whether or not she is the type of person who would more readily consent.

No male person under the age of fourteen can be guilty of this offence.

C-1

Landry was charged with rape in New Brunswick. The defence was that the girl involved had consented. After the evidence had been adduced and the judge had given his instructions to the jury, one of the members of the jury, speaking for several of their number, asked the trial judge, "If a man without the use of force works on the passions of a girl until such passions overcome the girl's unwillingness and she becomes willing for intercourse, would this consent be considered as having been given under force or of having been given freely?"

The trial judge instructed the jury that such consent would be considered as having been given under force.

Landry was convicted and appealed to the New Brunswick Court of

Appeal. The conviction was set aside on the grounds that the trial judge's reply to the juror's question was wrong and was a misdirection. A new trial was ordered.

      (a) Why was the judge's reply wrong?

C-2

Williams, a choirmaster, gave singing lessons to Vera, aged sixteen. On the occasion of one of her lessons, Williams said she was not singing properly and told her to lie down. He placed an instrument on the lower part of her body pretending to test her breathing. He then had sexual intercourse with the girl telling her he was making an air passage to improve her breathing. About three months later Williams repeated the performance. He was charged with rape and convicted. His appeal to the English Court of Appeal was dismissed.

      (a) Did Vera consent to intercourse? How was her consent obtained?

      (b) Why was Williams convicted?

Sexual Intercourse with a Female Under Fourteen

146. (1) Every male person who has sexual intercourse with a female person who
(a) is not his wife, and
(b) is under the age of fourteen years, whether or not he believes that she is fourteen years of age or more, is guilty of an indictable offence and is liable to imprisonment for life.

Sexual Intercourse with a Female Under Sixteen and Over Fourteen

146. (2) Every male person who has sexual intercourse with a female person who
(a) is not his wife,
(b) is of previously chaste character, and
(c) is fourteen years of age or more and is under the age of sixteen years,
whether or not he believes that she is sixteen years of age or more, is guilty of an indictable offence and is liable to imprisonment for five years.
(3) Where an accused is charged with an offence under subsection (2), the court may find the accused not guilty if it is of opinion that the evidence does not show that, as between the accused and the female person, the accused is more to blame than the female person.

Seduction of a Female Between Sixteen and Eighteen

> **151. Every male person who, being eighteen years of age or more, seduces a female person of previously chaste character who is sixteen years or more but less than eighteen years of age is guilty of an indictable offence and is liable to imprisonment for two years.**

The offence of rape under sections 143 and 144 protects females regardless of their age. The key element is the absence of consent. With respect to young girls, however, the law is even more concerned and makes it an offence for a male to have intercourse with such girls (other than one's wife) whether they consent or not.

With respect to girls under fourteen, the prohibition is total. Neither the fact that such a girl consents nor the fact that the male honestly believes her to be older is a defence to a charge of intercourse with a girl under fourteen.

With respect to girls over fourteen but under sixteen, the law is somewhat less stringent than with respect to girls under fourteen. Again, neither the fact that the girl consents nor an honest belief that she is older will constitute a defence. However, if it appears that the girl was (a) not of previously chaste character, or (b) the evidence does not show that the male was more to blame than the girl, the accused will be acquitted.

Section 151 dealing with girls between sixteen and eighteen continues the protection afforded young girls by the Criminal Code. However, as the potential penalty indicates, the level of protection is diminished. The female must be of previously chaste character and it must be the male who seduces her, i.e., leads the female astray. Again, consent is no defence.

There is a certain overlapping between the three previous offences and the offence of rape. For example:

if a male person has intercourse with a girl under fourteen and without her consent, he can be charged either with rape or with an offence contrary to section 146(1) of the Criminal Code. The prosecution will usually proceed under section 146(1) because it is easier to prove. (Consent is not an issue.) If, however, a girl under fourteen consents to intercourse, it cannot be rape and the charge must be laid under section 146(1).

While consent, mistake as to age, etc., do not constitute defences to the three foregoing offences, they are usually taken into consideration in determining the penalty. A male person under fourteen cannot be found guilty of either of the offences under section 146.

C-3

Johnston was charged at Kitchener with having sexual intercourse with a girl under the age of sixteen and over the age of fourteen. There was no question that the girl was under sixteen and that Johnston had intercourse with her. The sole issue was whether or not the girl was of previously chaste character. The trial judge, in giving his instructions to the jury, defined "chaste character" in terms of virginity. The jury returned a verdict of guilty. Johnston appealed to the Ontario Court of Appeal which set aside the conviction and directed a new trial. The Court of Appeal said that "chaste character" means "decent and clean in thoughts and conduct"—"moral cleanliness" and that chaste character and virginity were not necessarily the same.

> (a) Why are "chaste character" and "virginity" not necessarily the same?

Indecent Assault on a Female

> **149.   (1) Every one who indecently assaults a female person is guilty of an indictable offence and is liable to imprisonment for five years.**
> **(2) An accused who is charged with an offence under subsection (1) may be convicted if the evidence establishes that the accused did anything to the female person with her consent that, but for her consent, would have been an indecent assault, if her consent was obtained by false and fraudulent representations as to the nature and quality of the act.**

An indecent assault on a female involves two things: (a) an assault (see p. 27), i.e., a hostile act or threat and (b) circumstances of indecency. Both elements are necessary to constitute this offence. The most common form of the offence is a touching or attempt to touch the private parts of a female person, but any touching or attempt done in circumstances of indecency is an indecent assault. Circumstances of indecency may be inferred from all of the surrounding circumstances including words, gestures, etc. Ordinarily consent is a defence to this type of charge, for the obvious reason that a touching or striking with the consent of that person is not hostile and therefore not an assault. If, however, the consent was obtained by fraud [see subsection (2)], consent is not a defence, nor is the consent of a girl under fourteen a defence to a charge under this section.

C-4

Chong followed a fifteen-year-old girl on her way home. At a lonely spot he seized hold of her and offered her money to go with him for an immoral purpose. The girl cried out and threatened Chong with arrest. He let go of her and the girl ran home and complained to her father. Chong was arrested and charged with indecent assault. He was convicted by the magistrate and appealed to the Ontario Court of Appeal on the ground that there was nothing indecent in the way that he seized the girl and that at most he would be guilty of common assault. The appeal was dismissed. The court said that the assault could be interpreted by the surrounding circumstances, the words spoken, etc.

(a) What surrounding circumstances made the assault indecent?

C-5

Maurantonio posed as a doctor and purported to administer treatment to a number of women. In the course of the "treatment" he touched various parts of the bodies of those he treated. There was no evidence of any sexual advance to any of the women. Maurantonio was charged with indecent assault. It was argued by the defence that if the accused had been a doctor there would have been nothing in his conduct that would have made him guilty of indecent assault. Maurantonio was convicted and his conviction was affirmed by the Ontario Court of Appeal.

(a) Why was Maurantonio convicted of assault?

C-6

Beamish and M, a thirteen-year-old girl, went into the woods where they removed some of their clothes. With the consent of M, there was intimate body contact between them but no intercourse took place. Beamish was charged with indecent assault. He was acquitted by the Magistrate, but the decision was reversed by the Nova Scotia Court of Appeal.

(a) What do you think was the basis of the Magistrate's decision? Why was he wrong? Discuss.

Other Sexual Offences

The Criminal Code defines a number of other sexual offences, including indecent assault on a male person, gross indecency, incest, buggery and bestiality. However, as a result of a recent amendment to the Criminal Code, unnatural sexual practices and sexual relations between members of the same sex are no longer crimes if committed in private and between consenting adults.

Obscenity

As we have seen so far in this part, the Criminal Code defines certain sexual acts as crimes. These acts are capable of fairly exact definition and have traditionally been considered reprehensible. However, in the area of the transmission of imagery and ideas the problem of the criminal law becomes more difficult. The various forms of communication and entertainment media are increasingly occupied with sex, and their treatment of the subject becomes more and more explicit. Drawing the line between what might be considered art or literature and pornography is not always easy. Standards of tolerance vary from place to place and with changing times.

Obscene books, pictures, etc.

159.   (1) Every one commits an offence who
(a) makes, prints, publishes, distributes, circulates, or has in his possession for the purpose of publication, distribution or circulation any obscene written matter, picture, model, phonograph record or other thing whatsoever.

(2) Every one commits an offence who knowingly, without lawful justification or excuse,
(a) sells, exposes to public view or has in his possession for such a purpose any obscene written matter, picture, model, phonograph record or other thing whatsoever.

(6) Where an accused is charged with an offence under subsection (1) the fact that the accused was ignorant of the nature or presence of the matter, picture, model, phonograph record, crime comic or other thing by means of or in relation to which the offence was committed is not a defence to the charge.

(8) For the purposes of this Act, any publication a dominant characteristic of which is the undue exploitation of sex, or of sex and any one or more of the following subjects, namely, crime, horror, cruelty and violence, shall be deemed to be obscene.

In general terms, the object of this section is to make it a crime to make or distribute obscene material. Subsection (1) deals with those who are involved in a primary way—the maker, publisher, distributor, etc. Subsection (2) deals with the mere seller or person who exposes the material, e.g., the operator of a newsstand. A person charged under subsection (1) cannot use as a defence the fact that he did not know the nature of the material that he was dealing with. On the other hand, a person charged under subsection (2) must "knowingly sell, etc."

Porno, an obscene magazine, is handled by Worldwide News Service which distributes the magazine in Ontario. The magazine is retailed by a number of newsstands, one of which is Harry's newsstand. Neither the officials of Worldwide News nor Harry have ever read the magazine nor do they know what is in it. Worldwide is charged as a distributor under subsection (1); Harry is charged as a seller under subsection (2). Worldwide is guilty; Harry is not.

Subsection (8) now provides a definition of obscenity for offences under this section. However, the application of the definition remains difficult.

Anyone who commits either of the offences under this section is guilty of an indictable offence and is liable to imprisonment for two years or is guilty of an offence punishable on summary conviction.

C-7

In this case, the Supreme Court of Canada by a majority of five to four held that *Lady Chatterly's Lover* was not an obscene publication. The majority held that, measured by the inherent necessities of the novel itself, there was no undue exploitation of sex. The minority view was that the description in minute detail of Lady Chatterley's relationship with the gamekeeper made the dominant characteristic of the book the undue exploitation of sex.

C-8

The Ontario Court of Appeal was obliged to decide whether or not the novel *Fanny Hill—Memoirs of a Woman of Pleasure* by John Cleland was obscene. The court in a split decision, three to two, held that the book was not obscene. The book, a work of fiction, was a description by the principal character of her life as a prostitute. The court held that while sex was the dominant characteristic of the book, there was not an undue exploitation of sex in view of the subject matter of the book.

C-9

Great West News was charged with having possession of obscene written matter for the purpose of publication, distribution or circulation. The company distributed amongst other things the magazines *Film and Figure* and *Nude Living*. These magazines concentrated heavily upon showing nude female figures deliberately posed to reveal their genitalia. The company was convicted by a magistrate and an appeal to the Manitoba Court of Appeal was dismissed.

    (a) Compare the three previous cases. Why was the Great West case decided differently from the others?

    (b) Does the fact that a book largely deals with sex make it obscene?

C-10

Menkin was charged that he did have in his possession at Windsor for the purpose of sale certain obscene matter, namely a book entitled *Ten North Frederick,* contrary to section 159(2)(a) of the Criminal Code. Menkin operated a newsstand selling newspapers, magazines, and paperback books of all descriptions, among which was the book *Ten North Frederick.* Menkin testified that he had received no complaints about the book and had not read it himself. Without determining whether or not the book was obscene, the charge was dismissed.

    (a) Why was Menkin acquitted?

Obscene Theatrical Performances

> **163.   (1) Every one commits an offence who, being the lessee, manager, agent or person in charge of a theatre, presents or gives or allows to be presented or given there in an immoral, indecent or obscene performance, entertainment or representation.**
>
> **(2) Every one commits an offence who takes part or appears as an actor, performer, or assistant in any capacity, in an immoral, indecent or obscene performance, entertainment or representation in a theatre.**

Section 163 prohibits three types of performances—indecent, immoral, or obscene. While the terms are no doubt similar, the charge must be specific. Subsection (1) makes it a crime to be part of the production of such a performance. Subsection (2) makes it a crime to take part in the performance itself.

"Theatre" is defined by the Criminal Code to include any place that is open to the public where entertainment is given whether or not any charge is made for admission. The penalty for an offence under this section is the same as that for an offence under section 159.

C-11

Miss Johnson was charged in Calgary that she did unlawfully appear as a performer in an immoral performance, to wit, dancing in the nude in a theatre before a paying audience. On September 29, 1971, a detective of the Calgary police force went to a cabaret in Calgary and paid a $3.00 cover charge to be admitted. There were approximately 16 other paying guests present. There was a stage in the cabaret in front of which were approximately twenty tables. The stage was well lighted, Miss Johnson danced three dances scantily clad and then after a short intermission returned and performed a dance in the nude. She was alone on the stage and did nothing offensive by way of words or gestures while she danced. She was convicted by the magistrate who heard the charge. She appealed her conviction to a single judge of the Supreme Court of Alberta who reversed the conviction. The Crown then appealed to the Alberta Court of Appeal which restored the conviction. Miss Johnson in turn appealed to the Supreme Court of Canada and that court held in a split decision, six to three, that she should be acquitted on the grounds that the mere display of the human form was not immoral. The Supreme Court of Canada pointed out, however, that the charge against her was taking part in an *immoral* performance. They expressed no opinion as to what the result would have been if the charge had been taking part in an *indecent* performance.

    (a) Using a good dictionary look up the meaning of "immoral", "indecent", "obscene". Do you think that the conviction would have been upheld in the Supreme Court of Canada if the charge had been taking part in an "indecent" performance?

(b) What does the fact that the results swung back and forth from court to court suggest to you?

CASES FOR DISCUSSION

1. Bob, who is seventeen years of age, becomes attracted to Helen, an attractive fifteen-year-old girl who tells Bob that she is sixteen. Bob accepts this statement without question. One night after seeing a movie, Bob takes Helen home. Since her parents are not at home she invites him in. Sexual intercourse takes place. When Helen's father learns what has happened he goes to the police and Bob is charged with an offence contrary to section 146(2), (Intercourse with a girl over 14 and under 16).

(a) Is Bob guilty or not? Explain.

2. Farley Filbert writes a novel called *Cold Charity* which deals with the story of a family who migrates to Canada from South America. Part of the story concerns the daughter Maria who is seduced by her employer. She then begins selling her favours to her employer and others to help support the family. The seduction and her subsequent activities are described in explicit detail. The book becomes a best seller. The publisher is charged with publishing obscene written matter contrary to section 159(1) of the Criminal Code.

(a) Is the publisher guilty or not? Explain.

3. Marcia goes to a party at a summer cottage. The party becomes rather wild and a great deal of drinking takes place. Marcia eventually passes out; some of her friends carry her to one of the bedrooms and place her on the bed. Later, Danny enters the room and has sexual intercourse with the unconscious Marcia. When Marcia regains consciousness she is told what happened. She goes to the police and Danny is charged with rape.

(a) Is he guilty or not? Explain.

4. Susan is taking swimming lessons at the high school pool and is wearing a very brief bikini. The lower part of the suit is secured by being tied in a bow at each side. As she stands at the edge of the pool, David, who is also taking lessons, sneaks up behind her and pulls both bows loose causing the lower part of her suit to fall. Susan, extremely embarrassed, runs from the area to the changing room. David is called to the principal's office and is told that this type of conduct could constitute an indecent assault.

(a) Do you agree? Discuss.

PART FIVE
OFFENCES AGAINST PUBLIC ORDER

All crimes are offences against the State and in that sense may be said to be offences against public order. However, in most cases the involvement of the public is not obvious.

> Sykes steals Jones' car. The immediate victim is Jones but the public is involved because Sykes has endangered the right of everyone to live peacefully and own private property.

In some offences, however, the danger to the whole of society is obvious and direct. In this type of offence there is usually no single victim—the offender confronts the whole community. The offence can range from the extremely serious (treason) to the relatively minor (creating a disturbance by shouting).

Treason

46.   (1) Every one commits treason who, in Canada,

(a) kills or attempts to kill Her Majesty, or does her any bodily harm tending to death or destruction, maims or wounds her, or imprisons or restrains her;

(b) levies war against Canada or does any act preparatory thereto;

(c) assists an enemy at war with Canada, or any armed forces against whom Canadian Forces are engaged in hostilities whether or not a state of war exists between Canada and the country whose forces they are;

(d) uses force or violence for the purpose of overthrowing the government of Canada or a province;

(e) without lawful authority, communicates or makes available to an agent of a state other than Canada, military or scientific information or any sketch, plan, model, article, note or document of a military or scientific character that he knows or ought to know may be used by that state for a purpose prejudicial to the safety or defence of Canada;

(f) conspires with any person to do anything mentioned in paragraphs (a) to (d);

(g) forms an intention to do anything mentioned in paragraphs (a) to (d) and manifests that intention by an overt act; or

(h) conspires with any person to do anything mentioned in paragraph (e) or forms an intention to do anything mentioned in paragraph (e) and manifests that intention by an overt act.

(2) Notwithstanding subsection (1), a Canadian citizen or a person who owes allegiance to Her Majesty in right of Canada commits treason if, while in or out of Canada, he does anything mentioned in subsection (1).

(3) Where it is treason to conspire with any person, the act of conspiring is an overt act of treason.

47.   (1) Every one who commits treason is guilty of an indictable offence and is liable

(a) to be sentenced to death if he is guilty of an offence under paragraph 46(1) (a), (b) or (c);

(b) to be sentenced to death or to imprisonment for life if he is guilty of an offence under paragraph 46(1) (d), (f) or (g);

(c) to be sentenced to death or to imprisonment for life if he is guilty of an offence under paragraph 46(1) (e) or (h), committed while a state of war exists between Canada and another country; or

(d) to be sentenced to imprisonment for fourteen years if he is guilty of an offence under paragraph 46(1) (e) or (h), committed while no state of war exists between Canada and another country.

These sections of the Code embody, with some statutory modifications, the ancient principles that a citizen or anyone who owes allegiance to a country should not do anything to destroy or harm that country. Even aliens have a duty to do nothing to harm or destroy a country while they are in it. Section 46 sets out the specific items which will constitute treason if committed in Canada by anyone, whether or not he is a citizen or alien or whether or not he owes any allegiance to Canada. With respect to Canadian citizens or anyone who owes allegiance to Canada, section 46(2) makes any of the acts referred to in subsection (1) treason, even if committed outside of Canada.

C-1

DeJager lived in Waschbank in Natal, South Africa, a British colony. During the Boer War the British forces lost control of Waschbank, which was taken over by the Boer forces for about six months. During that period DeJager assisted and aided the Boer forces as a commissioner and justice of the peace. Later DeJager was charged with treason. He argued that when Waschbank was occupied by the Boers he was no longer under the protection of the British government and was obliged to perform certain duties for the occupying forces. DeJager was convicted. His appeal was dismissed on the grounds that his duty to the British government did not cease because of the temporary withdrawal of British forces.

(a) If this case had happened in Canada, what part of section 46 would apply?

(b) Do you agree that the performance of duties helpful to an occupying army should be classed as treason?

C-2

Joyce was born in the U.S.A. in 1906, thereby becoming a natural-born American citizen. At the age of three he was taken to Ireland, where he stayed until 1921. He then moved to England, where he remained until 1939. In 1933 he applied for and obtained a British passport. In August of 1939 he applied for a renewal of the passport which was renewed until July 1, 1940.

With the outbreak of war in September 1939, Joyce left England and went to Germany where he broadcast propaganda from Germany to England from September to December of 1939. After the war Joyce was arrested and charged with treason. He was convicted and appealed his conviction to the House of Lords on the grounds that what he had done took place outside the United Kingdom and that he was not a British subject nor did he owe any allegiance to the United Kingdom. His appeal was dismissed on the grounds that since he held a British passport, he owed allegiance to the British Crown.

(a) What part of section 46 would apply to Joyce's conduct?

(b) If Joyce had not performed his broadcasting until July 2, 1941, would he have been guilty of treason?

C-3

A large number of armed men described as Fenians crossed from Buffalo, New York, to Fort Erie, Ontario, in June 1866. Slavin, an American citizen, crossed over a little later and spent the night with the invaders. The next day the invaders were met by Canadian troops and driven out of the country. Slavin was seen carrying a rifle and bayonet similar to those carried by the invaders. Slavin stated that he had found the rifle on the road.

Slavin was captured and charged with treason. He said he had no intention of levying war against Her Majesty and while he had been with the Fenians he was not one of them. The jury did not accept this explanation. Slavin was convicted and his appeal was dismissed.

(a) Would you have been convinced beyond a reasonable doubt that Slavin intended to levy war against Canada?

(b) What other parts of Section 46 would have justified a conviction?

Unlawful Assemblies and Riots

64.   (1) An unlawful assembly is an assembly of three or more persons who, with intent to carry out any common purpose, assemble in such a manner or so conduct themselves when they are assembled as to cause persons in the neighbourhood of the assembly to fear, on reasonable grounds, that they

(a) will disturb the peace tumultuously, or

(b) will by that assembly needlessly and without reasonable cause provoke other persons to disturb the peace tumultuously.

> **(2) Persons who are lawfully assembled may become an unlawful assembly if they conduct themselves with a common purpose in a manner that would have made the assembly unlawful if they had assembled in that manner for that purpose.**
>
> **(3) Persons are not unlawfully assembled by reason only that they are assembled to protect the dwelling-house of any one of them against persons who are threatening to break and enter it for the purpose of committing an indictable offence therein.**
> **65. A riot is an unlawful assembly that has begun to disturb the peace tumultuously.**
> **66. Every one who takes part in a riot is guilty of an indictable offence and is liable to imprisonment for two years.**
> **67. Every one who is a member of an unlawful assembly is guilty of an offence punishable on a summary conviction.**

The Canadian Bill of Rights guarantees to everyone the right to freedom of assembly and association. However, the assembly and association must be peaceable and in conformance with the criminal law. The above sections define two offences, firstly being a member of an unlawful assembly and secondly, taking part in a riot. Section 64 defines an unlawful assembly as one which will cause persons in the neighbourhood to fear that there will be a tumultuous disturbance of the peace. A riot occurs when the unlawful assembly has actually begun to disturb the peace tumultuously.

Tumultuously is a fairly broad term but means "full of commotion, disorder or turbulence."

C-4

In 1931 in Hamilton, Ontario, there were a great many men unemployed. Patterson assumed a position of leadership among them. They arranged to parade to demonstrate the extent of the unemployment and attract public support. There was no suggestion that they intended to break the law.

On the day set for the parade about 800 men assembled and began to march. A number of police officers escorted the parade. When they reached the central downtown area, the police asked them to turn one way or the other and not proceed into that area since a permit was required to parade there. (A permit had been applied for earlier but had been refused.) Earlier Patterson had told the group that he would lead them into the prohibited area and they should follow. He then led the group into the forbidden area and a great deal of pushing and shoving took place, the crowd became quite unmanageable, and traffic was tied up in all directions. Patterson was charged with being a member of an unlawful assembly and was convicted. He appealed to the Ontario Court of Appeal which in a split decision, three to two, upheld the conviction. The majority of the Court stated:

> **No matter how worthy the cause or how clear the right to be asserted may be, our law requires the worthy cause to be advo-**

cated and the right to be asserted in a peaceable way and not by riot and tumult. The provision of the Code prohibiting unlawful assembly is for the purpose of drawing the line between a lawful meeting and an assembly either unlawful in its inception or which is deemed to have become unlawful either by reason of the action of those who assembled or by reason of the improper action of others having no sympathy with the objects of the meeting.

(a) Do you agree with the majority decision of the Ontario Court of Appeal? Read again the definition of "unlawful assembly" contained in the Criminal Code.

C-5

In 1932, members of an association in Rouyn, Quebec, asked the municipal authorities for permission to have a public meeting on the City Hall grounds. Permission was refused. A few days later the meeting was held by the association outside their own association hall. About 150 people attended in front of the building. The space between the building and the sidewalk was not large enough to accommodate the crowd, so many stood on the sidewalk preventing passage of others. A speaker opened the meeting from the front porch of the building. The police arrived and ordered the crowd to disperse. The speaker then addressed the meeting asking if he should speak outside or inside. The crowd replied, "Inside." A few arrests were made and some of the crowd began to throw rocks at the policemen. One officer was injured. The crowd refused to disperse and a fire hose was turned on them. Members of the crowd cut the hose and the crowd threatened to take possession of the police station. The police fired their revolvers in the air and the crowd dispersed.

Pavletich and thirty-two others who participated in the meeting and who threw stones and refused to leave were charged with being members of an unlawful assembly. A Quebec magistrate convicted Pavletich.

(a) Was the meeting unlawful in the beginning?
(b) Did the meeting become unlawful? If so, when?

C-6

A large number of young people occupied the Beatty Street Armory in Vancouver as a hostel during the summer of 1970. On September 10 the hostel at the armory was closed and the occupants moved to the Jericho Armed Forces Base in Vancouver. On October 15 the arrangement at the Armed Forces Base was terminated and the occupants evicted. The occupants left the base but remained on the roadway outside the gate and immediate area. During the afternoon the crowd grew to about 250. The police addressed the crowd by loudspeaker and asked them to clear the roadway and let traffic through. The response from the crowd contained obscenities and abuse of the police. At 5:15 p.m. the crowd was asked to disperse within five minutes and the crowd refused. As a result, about twenty-five police officers advanced in a line to clear the crowd. The crowd then began to retreat to the grass of the Jericho Hill School, a school for deaf and blind children. The children were in school at the time and some went to the windows to watch. As the crowd retreated, rocks were thrown at the police and three or four officers were struck. Thomas, one of the demonstrators, had stated that the demonstrators were not going anywhere and had scattered roofing nails on the road in front of the police motor-cycles. Thomas was charged with taking part in a riot. A British Columbia County Court Judge held that whatever grievance the crowd had about the hostel arrangements, it did not justify their conduct and there was an unlawful assembly. He, however, had a reasonable doubt as to whether or not the unlawful assembly had begun to disturb the peace tumultuously so as to constitute a riot. He therefore acquitted Thomas of taking part in a riot but convicted him of the lesser offence of being a member of an unlawful assembly.

    (a) What is the difference between an unlawful assembly and a riot?

    (b) Do you agree with the decision in this case?

Reading the Riot Act

68.   A justice, mayor or sheriff or the lawful deputy of a mayor or sheriff who receives notice that, at any place within his jurisdiction, twelve or more persons are unlawfully and riotously assembled together, shall go to that place and, after approaching as near as safely he may do, if he is satisfied that a riot is in progress, shall command silence and thereupon make or cause to be made in a loud voice a proclamation in the following words or to the like effect:

Her Majesty the Queen charges and commands all persons being assembled immediately to disperse and peaceably to depart to their habitations or to their lawful business upon the pain of being guilty of an offence for which, upon conviction, they may be sentenced to imprisonment for life. GOD SAVE THE QUEEN.

69.   Every one is guilty of an indictable offence and is liable to imprisonment for life who

(a) opposes, hinders or assaults, wilfully and with force, a person who begins to make or is about to begin to make or is making the proclamation referred to in section 68 so to that it is not made,

(b) does not peaceably disperse and depart from a place where the proclamation referred to in section 68 is made within thirty minutes after it is made, or

(c) does not depart from a place within thirty minutes when he has reasonable ground to believe that the proclamation referred to in section 68 would have been made in that place if some person had not opposed, hindered or assaulted, wilfully and with force, a person who would have made it.

The Riot Act passed in England in 1715 introduced the form of proclamation contained in section 68 and the reading of this section is ordinarily referred to as reading the Riot Act. The purpose of reading the proclamation is to warn rioters of the extreme gravity of their position. Interfering with the reading of the proclamation is itself an extremely serious offence, and failure to disperse within one-half hour after the proclamation is read or is attempted to be read becomes a very serious offence, as well.

The fact that the half hour time limit is imposed does not mean that no action may be taken earlier; it simply means that the offence becomes much more serious if the rioters do not disperse within that time.

Obstructing a Police Officer

> **118.** **Every one who**
> **(a) resists or wilfully obstructs a public officer or peace officer in the execution of his duty or any person lawfully acting in aid of such an officer,**
> **(b) omits, without reasonable excuse, to assist a public officer or peace officer in the execution of his duty in arresting a person or in preserving the peace, after having reasonable notice that he is required to do so, or**
> **(c) resists or wilfully obstructs any person in the lawful execution of a process against lands or goods or in making a lawful distress or seizure,**
> **is guilty of**
> **(d) an indictable offence and is liable to imprisonment for two years, or**
> **(e) an offence punishable on summary conviction.**

The terms "peace officer" and "public officer" in general include anyone charged with the enforcement of the law, including police officers, sheriffs, sheriff's officers, prison guards, members of the armed forces, customs and immigration officers, etc. The task of those charged with the enforcement of the law is usually difficult enough in itself without being made more difficult by someone interfering. As a result, the Criminal Code makes it an offence for anyone to resist or wilfully obstruct an officer in the execution of his duty. Subsection (b) also makes it an offence for anyone to omit without reasonable excuse to assist an officer in the execution of his duty. "Obstructing" is not defined in the Criminal Code, but generally means "to hinder, oppose or block". Charges under subsection (a) are relatively common, whereas charges under subsection (b) are rare. Members of the public are not often called upon by public officers to assist actively.

C-7
In 1971, Premier Kosygin of the U.S.S.R. was to visit Edmonton as a part of an official visit to Canada. He was scheduled to stop briefly at the

Chateau Lacombe Hotel in Edmonton. A few days earlier in Ottawa a man pushed through the crowd and assaulted the Premier. As a result of this, before Premier Kosygin arrived in Edmonton, twenty-five police officers cordoned off an area in front of the hotel. Knowlton wished to enter the cordoned-off area to take a picture but was warned by the police to stay out. He refused to heed the warning and pushed his way between two police constables into the restricted area, just before Premier Kosygin was schedduled to arrive. Knowlton was arrested and charged with wilfully obstructing an officer in the execution of his duty. Knowlton's defence was that the police had no right to interfere with his free access to public streets and, therefore, they were not in the execution of their duty. The provincial judge who heard the case accepted this argument and the charge was dismissed. The Alberta Court of Appeal reversed the decision and Knowlton was convicted. An appeal by Knowlton to the Supreme Court of Canada was dismissed. Both Appellate Courts held that the police had a duty to protect visiting dignitaries and that Knowlton was obstructing the officers in the performance of that duty.

> (a) In what way did Knowlton's conduct obstruct the officers in the performance of their duty?

C-8

Two police officers had been directed to work in plain clothes in the skid row area of Vancouver. Westlie, who knew the identity of the two officers, began shouting, "Undercover pigs, undercover fuzz, watch out for the pigs." One of the officers told Westlie that they were on duty and warned him to stop. Westlie continued, stopping people on the street, pointing to the officers referring to them as "undercover pigs," "undercover fuzz." Westlie was charged with obstructing an officer in the execution of his duty. He was convicted by the Provincial Judge and appealed to the British Columbia Court of Appeal. The defence argued that the police officers were not performing any specific duty and in any event, Westlie was not obstructing or interfering with the police officers. The appeal was dismissed. The British Columbia Court of Appeal held that the police officers were on general patrol to prevent crime and apprehend offenders and that Westlie was interfering with the performance of that duty.

> (a) How did the conduct of Westlie obstruct the officers in the performance of their duty?

Causing a Disturbance

> **171.** **Every one who**
> **(a) not being in a dwelling-house causes a disturbance in or near a public place,**
> **(i) by fighting, screaming, shouting, swearing, singing or using insulting or obscene language,**
> **(ii) by being drunk, or**

> **(iii) by impeding or molesting other persons,**
> **(b) openly exposes or exhibits an indecent exhibition in a public place,**
> **(c) loiters in a public place and in any way obstructs persons who are there, or**
> **(d) disturbs the peace and quiet of the occupants of a dwelling-house by discharging firearms or by other disorderly conduct in a public place or who, not being an occupant of a dwelling-house comprised in a particular building or structure, disturbs the peace and quiet of the occupants of a dwelling-house comprised in the building or structure by discharging firearms or by other disorderly conduct in any part of a building or structure to which, at the time of such conduct, the occupants of two or more dwelling houses comprised in the building or structure have access as of right or by invitation, express or implied,**
> **is guilty of an offence punishable on summary conviction.**

This section covers a wide area of conduct which disturbs public order. Charges are commonly laid under section 171(a) charging persons with causing a disturbance by fighting. The evil aimed at is not the fight but the disturbance caused by the attraction of a crowd and the public disorder. Subsection (d) contains the well known offence of disturbing the peace. The disturbing of the peace can take place by discharging firearms or by "other disorderly conduct" in a public place, or those parts of private buildings that are used in common with others. Generally speaking, the prohibitions contained in section 171 are limited to public places. Disturbances in private places are sometimes covered by municipal by-laws or are dealt with in civil law suits.

C-9

On the morning of August 10, 1970, Goddard was assisting in directing a legal picket line at a plant where a strike was in progress. A bus arrived containing a group of workers who wished to enter the plant. Goddard and others continued to walk back and forth across the entrance preventing the bus from entering. The driver and passengers remained in the bus. At the end of about ten minutes Goddard was arrested, the other picketers broke up, and the bus entered. Goddard was charged with causing a disturbance by impeding other persons. There was no evidence of any noise or commotion. Goddard was convicted by a Provincial Court Judge who was of the opinion that the conduct of the accused might have provoked reprisal and was, therefore, a disturbance. On appeal to a Judge of the Supreme Court of Ontario, the conviction was set aside on the grounds that the disturbance must be a public disturbance and that a mental disturbance or annoyance is not the kind of disturbance contemplated by this section.

> (a) Assume that the passengers had left the bus and begun to mill around. Would the result of this case have been any different? Why?

C-10

On March 10, 1969, two employees of Plasticast Limited left the company premises in a car. At the time a strike was in progress. Sturdevant and another who were on picket duty stood in the driveway refusing to move and thereby forcing the car to stop. The police were called ten minutes later but before the police arrived Sturdevant and his companion stood aside. There was no commotion between the occupants of the car and Sturdevant, nor did the occupants get out of the car. Sturdevant was charged with causing a disturbance by impeding. The Provincial Judge who tried the case dismissed the charge.

> (a) Why was the charge dismissed?
> (b) Do you agree or disagree with the result?

C-11

In the early morning of October 15, 1967, Emms and a companion entered the lobby of a hotel in Nipawin, Saskatchewan. A night clerk was on duty and Emms lodged a verbal attack on the night clerk for some ten or fifteen minutes, using such words as "son of a bitch", "old bastard", "f—— you". As a result of the commotion, guests were disturbed. Emms was charged with "unlawfully causing a disturbance by swearing contrary to the Criminal Code." Emms was convicted by a magistrate and appealed to a District Court Judge. The appeal was successful. The District Court Judge held that swearing is the employment of an oath in a manner contemptuous or irreverent of God.

> (a) Why was the language used not swearing?
> (b) Would the result have been different if Emms had been charged with (1) causing a disturbance by using obscene language, (2) causing a disturbance by using insulting language?

CASES FOR DISCUSSION

1. The authorities in your area decide to close down the high school which you are attending because of the age of the building and distribute the students between two neighbouring high schools. The student body is very much upset and feelings run high. A protest march is planned culminating in an assembly in front of the school where speeches will be made.

> (a) What factors must be kept in mind in planning such a demonstration?
> (b) What precautions should be taken?
> (c) What should the participants be told about the possibility of criminal prosecution?

2. On the night of graduation from grade 13, the class stages a party at the home of one of the graduates. At 4 o'clock in the morning, loud and

raucous singing continues to shatter the night air. Neighbours call the police who arrive to find a group of five on the sidewalk in front of the house enthusiastically performing the school football cheers. The rest of the group is in the house singing.

> (a) Can charges be laid under section 171? If so, what specific charge can be laid and against whom?

3.   Constable Bauer, while on patrol, sees a man snatch a purse from a woman on the street. The woman shouts for help and Bauer runs after the thief. The thief then gets into a car and speeds off. Bauer, seeing Green who has just drawn up to the curb in a car, jumps in Green's car and tells Green to follow the thief's car. Green refuses. He says that he just bought the car and doesn't want to run the risk of damaging it.

> (a) Has Green committed a criminal offence? Explain in full.

4.   Fred and several companions are lounging around the central corridor of the Bargain Town Shopping Mall. A security officer asks Fred to leave and Fred refuses, using obscene language. A crowd gathers as the officer repeats his order to Fred to leave. Fred again answers using obscene language and then leaves the store premises. A few days later Fred receives a summons charging him with "causing a disturbance by using obscene language."

> (a) Is he guilty? Discuss.

PART SIX
OFFENCES INVOLVING DRUGS

The criminal law with respect to drugs is found in two federal statutes, the Narcotic Control Act and the Food and Drugs Act. Both of these Acts provide for authorization of the drugs they cover for legitimate purposes, e.g., medical and scientific, but provide for offences outside of the authorized uses.

Narcotics

The Narcotic Control Act defines "narcotic" to include a large number of substances, their derivatives and salts. The most commonly known of these substances are opium, codeine, morphine, cocaine, marihuana (cannabis), hashish (cannabis resin), methadols, and benzazocines. The Act provides several offences as follows:

Possession

> **3.   (1) Except as authorized by this Act or the regulation, no person shall have a narcotic in his possession.**
>
> **(2) Every person who violates subsection (1) is guilty of an indictable offence and is liable**
>> **(a) upon summary conviction for a first offence, to a fine of one thousand dollars or to imprisonment for six months or to both fine and imprisonment, and for a subsequent offence, to a fine of two thousand dollars or to imprisonment for one year or to both fine and imprisonment; or**
>> **(b) upon conviction on indictment, to imprisonment for seven years.**

This is the most common offence for which charges are laid under the Narcotic Control Act, the simple act of having possession of the prohibited substance. The Narcotic Control Act, however, adopts the definition of "possession" contained in the Criminal Code which enlarges the meaning of what is ordinarily considered possession. The Criminal Code provides:

> **(a) a person has anything in possession when he has it in his personal possession or knowingly**
>> **(i) has it in the actual possession or custody of another person, or**
>> **(ii) has it in any place, whether or not that place belongs to or is occupied by him, for the use or benefit of himself or another person; and**
>
> **(b) where one of two or more persons, with the knowledge and consent of the rest, has anything in his custody or possession, it shall be deemed to be in the custody and possession of each and all of them.**

C-1

Beaver sold a package containing a narcotic (diacetylmorphine) to an undercover police agent and was charged with possession of a narcotic. The defence was that the accused did not know that the package contained morphine and thought it was sugar of milk. The trial judge held that it did not matter whether or not Beaver knew what the substance was in the package or whether he had mistaken belief as to what the substance was, and found him guilty. The Supreme Court of Canada set aside the verdict and directed a new trial holding that there could be no possession without knowledge of the character of the forbidden substance.

(a) Do you agree with this decision? Why or why not?

(b) If a friend asks you to hold his lunch for a few minutes and the bag contains a narcotic, can you be guilty of possession?

C-2

Overvold was arrested and charged with possession of a narcotic. A microscopic examination of a pipe in the possession of the accused revealed minute traces of cannabis resin. There was no other evidence. The charge was dismissed.

    (a) Compare this case with *R. v. Beaver*. Is there a common principle involved?

    (b) Assume that Overvold knew there was a microscopic trace of marihuana in the pipe. Should he be convicted?

C-3

On February 1, 1969, an MG sportscar was stopped outside St. John, New Brunswick, by the RCMP. The driver of the car was one V. and sitting beside him was Harvey. Both were searched and no narcotics or drugs were found on them. The car was searched and under the mat in front of the gear shift was found a quantity of marihuana. The police also found a small amount of marihuana on the floor directly in front of and one inch ahead of the seat in which Harvey had been sitting. Harvey was charged with possession of marihuana. He denied any knowledge of the marihuana. Harvey was convicted by the magistrate who was of the opinion that V. was in possession of the narcotic since it was his car. The magistrate further held that Harvey knew that V. had possession of the marihuana and because of the extended definition of "possession", Harvey was also in possession of marihuana. The New Brunswick Court of Appeal reversed the conviction of Harvey holding that "knowledge and consent" in the extended definition cannot exist without some measure of control and there was no evidence that Harvey had any measure of control over the marihuana.

    (a) If the marihuana had been found on the bucket seat occupied by Harvey, would the result have been different? Why or why not?

Trafficking—Possession for the Purpose of Trafficking

    (4)   **(1) No person shall traffic in a narcotic or any substance represented or held out by him to be a narcotic.**

    (2) No person shall have in his possession any narcotic for the purpose of trafficking.

    (3) Every person who violates subsection (1) or (2) is guilty of indictable offence and is liable to imprisonment for life.

"Trafficking" is defined to mean "manufacture, sell, give, administer, transport, send, deliver or distribute". This section creates two distinct offences:

(a) trafficking, which contemplates the commission of the very act of trafficking by the accused and

(b) possession for any purpose of trafficking.

To constitute the latter offence, it is not necessary that the accused actually commit the act of trafficking, but simply have possession of a narcotic for that purpose. In a prosecution for this offence, once the Crown has proved possession of a narcotic, the accused must show his purpose was something other than trafficking. The purpose can be ascertained from the quantity of the narcotic, the surrounding circumstances, what the accused says, etc.

C-4

An undercover member of the RCMP asked Larson if he knew where he could buy an ounce of hashish. Larson said he would enquire. He returned saying that he could get an ounce for $60.00 or $70.00 and that he wanted one gram of hashish in return for getting him the ounce. The two proceeded to an address in West Vancouver. The RCMP officer gave Larson $75.00 for the hashish, telling him to get a gram for himself. Larson then entered the house and returned with the hashish. Later Larson was arrested and charged with trafficking. Larson testified that he did not help sell the hashish nor did he have any connection whatever with the seller, but that he simply bought on behalf of the RCMP officer. He was convicted of trafficking and the conviction was upheld by the British Columbia Court of Appeal.

(a) Why did Larson's action constitute trafficking?

Importing

(5)   (1) Except as authorized by this Act or the regulations, no person shall import into Canada or export from Canada any narcotic.

(2) Every person who violates subsection (1) is guilty of an indictable offence and is liable to imprisonment for life but not less than seven years.

Cultivation

(6)   (1) No person shall cultivate opium poppy or marihuana except under authority of and in accordance with a licence issued to him under the regulations.

(2) Every person who violates subsection (1) is guilty of an indictable offence and is liable to imprisonment for seven years.

(3) The Minister* may cause to be destroyed any growing

*The Minister of National Health and Welfare.

**plant of opium poppy or marihuana cultivated otherwise than
under authority of and in accordance with a licence issued under
the regulations.**

These two sections are self-explanatory but it will be observed that section
5 is one of the few instances where a minimum sentence is prescribed.

C-5

Geesman flew from Spain to Dorval Airport, Montreal. After disembarking
from the aircraft he was checked by the customs authorities who detained
him for a more detailed examination. He was searched and ten pounds of
hashish were found strapped to his body. The accused was arrested and
charged with importing a narcotic into Canada. The accused testified that
he was in transit on his way to the United States and did not intend to dis-
pose of the hashish in Canada and as a result had no intention of importing
the hashish into Canada. Geesman was convicted by a Quebec judge of the
Sessions of the Peace and sentenced to the minimum term of seven years.

    (a) Why was Geesman convicted?
    (b) Why was his intention "not to import hashish into Canada"
        disregarded?

Controlled and Restricted Drugs

The Food and Drugs Act sets up two classes of drugs, controlled and restricted
drugs. Provision is made for authorized use of both classes and offences are
defined for use outside of the authorized uses.

    "*Controlled drug*" is defined to include Amphetamine, Barbituric acid,
Benzphetamine, Methamphetamine, their derivatives and salts. Except as
authorized by the Food and Drugs Act, or the regulations thereunder, it is an
offence to traffic in a controlled drug or to have possession of a controlled
drug for the purpose of trafficking. The penalty for both these offences is the
same. A person convicted of either of these offences is liable on summary
conviction to imprisonment for eighteen months or on conviction on indictment to imprisonment for ten years.

    "*Restricted drug*" is defined to include a number of drugs with lengthy
chemical names, the short forms of which are LSD, DET, DMT, STP (DOM),
MDA, LBJ, their derivatives and salts. It is an offence to have unauthorized
possession of a restricted drug. Unauthorized possession of a restricted drug
renders the offender liable on summary conviction to a fine of $1000 or six
months' imprisonment or both. The same offence on indictment renders the

offender liable to a fine of $5,000 or imprisonment for three years or both. Trafficking or possession for the purpose of trafficking in a restricted drug are offences rendering the offender liable on summary conviction to eighteen months' imprisonment or on indictment to imprisonment for ten years.

CASES FOR DISCUSSION

1. The RCMP raid Black's apartment and find two pounds of marihuana, three packages of cigarette papers, a small scale, two packages of plastic "baggies". Black is charged with the possession of a narcotic for the purpose of trafficking.

    (a) What procedure is followed at the trial?
    (b) Black testifies that he had the marihuana for his own use. In your opinion is he guilty of possession for the purpose of trafficking? Why or why not?

2. Arthurs rents a car in Detroit, Michigan, and drives it across the bridge to Windsor, Ontario. He is stopped by the Customs officers who search the car. Concealed inside the door panel the officers find a plastic bag containing ten grams of heroin. Arthurs is charged with importing a narcotic into Canada.

    (a) Is he guilty? Why or why not?

3. Four young people decide to experiment with marihuana and each contributes five dollars to one of their number who takes the twenty dollars and purchases a small quantity of marihuana. Before the purchaser returns to join his companions he is arrested and charged with possession of a narcotic. When the police learn the facts, they also charge his three friends with the same offence.

    (a) Are they guilty? Why or why not?

DISCUSSION

1. Many argue that marihuana should be classified as a restricted or controlled drug rather than a narcotic.
    (a) What difference would this make? Do you agree or not?

2. The Ledain Commission on the non-medical use of drugs has recommended that known drug addicts be taken into custody and given treatment whether or not they consent.
    (a) Do you agree? What dangers are contained in this recommendation?

PART SEVEN
OFFENCES INVOLVING THE USE OF AN AUTOMOBILE

All of the provinces have statutes dealing with the operation of motor vehicles regarding their use, equipment, ownership, etc. Contravention of these laws usually involves a fine or, in some cases, a jail term. Even municipalities are empowered to pass by-laws dealing with some forms of traffic, parking, etc., and contravention of these by-laws involves a penalty.

The federal government has seen fit to classify some forms of conduct in the operation of a motor vehicle sufficiently serious and dangerous to the public to be criminal.

Criminal Negligence

> **203. Every one who by criminal negligence causes death to another person is guilty of an indictable offence and is liable to imprisonment for life.**
> **204. Every one who by criminal negligence causes bodily harm to another person is guilty of an indictable offence and is liable to imprisonment for ten years.**
> **233. (1) Every one who is criminally negligent in the operation of a motor vehicle is guilty of**
> > **(a) an indictable offence and is liable to imprisonment for five years, or**
> > **(b) an offence punishable on summary conviction.**

Sections 203 and 204 are sections of general application in the Criminal Code and are not confined to the operation of motor vehicles but obviously cover the criminally negligent operation of a motor vehicle where death is caused (203) or bodily harm is caused (204). Section 233(1) makes it an offence to operate a motor vehicle in a manner that is criminally negligent whether or not any particular result is caused.

A person is criminally negligent who, in doing anything, or omitting to do anything that it is his duty to do, shows wanton or reckless disregard for the lives or safety of other persons. Example:

> McDonald drives his automobile at 75 miles per hour on a city street running through several stop signs and automatic signal lights. If he is apprehended he is charged under 233(1). If he causes an accident and injures someone he may be charged under 204. If his driving causes death he can be charged under 203.

Dangerous Driving

> **233. (4) Every one who drives a motor vehicle on a street, road, highway or other public place in a manner that is dangerous to the public, having regard to all the circumstances includ-**

ing the nature, condition and use of such place and the amount of traffic that at the time is or might reasonably be expected to be on such place, is guilty of
    (a) an indictable offence and is liable to imprisonment for two years, or
    (b) an offence punishable on summary conviction.

This offence is similar to the offence of criminal negligence in the operation of a motor vehicle but dangerous driving is a less serious offence. The definition is much broader and covers negligent conduct that would not amount to criminal negligence. To constitute dangerous driving, the conduct need not be wanton or willful. It has been held that while the definition of dangerous driving is very wide, it does not cover conduct that is mere inadvertent negligence.

C-1

Northam was driving a car northerly on a street in Calgary at about 11:40 p.m. The street was a one-way street for northbound traffic. At an intersection the vehicle driven by Northam struck a pedestrian who was in the north crosswalk proceeding westerly. The vehicle stopped 200 feet past the point of impact, having dragged the pedestrian about 94 feet. The pedestrian died. Northam was charged with criminal negligence causing death. The evidence indicated that Northam's vehicle was exceeding the speed limit of 30 miles per hour but by how much was not entirely clear. The pedestrian was wearing dark clothing. A lighting expert testified that a pedestrian so clothed would be difficult to see because the background was dark. At trial the accused was acquitted of criminal negligence causing death but convicted of dangerous driving. Both the Crown and the defence appealed. The Alberta Court of Appeal upheld the dismissal of the criminal negligence but reversed the conviction on the dangerous driving charge and acquitted the accused.

    (a) Why did the trial court acquit Northam of criminal negligence causing death?
    (b) Why did the Appeal Court acquit Northam of dangerous driving?
    (c) How would you classify the manner in which the car was driven?

C-2

On February 24, 1969, Sutherland was driving a car northerly on Douglas Street in Saanich, British Columbia. For about two miles the car had been travelling in an erratic manner and then veered into the southbound lane colliding with a motorcycle and then a fence on the west side of the road. Sutherland had been up most of the night before and had fallen asleep at the wheel. He was charged with dangerous driving and convicted in Magistrate's Court. The Magistrate was of the opinion that the facts showed driving that was more than inadvertent negligence.

> (a) Compare this case with *R. v. Northam*. Do you agree that Sutherland should have been convicted?

Leaving the Scene

> **233.   (2) Every one who, having the care, charge or control of a vehicle that is involved in an accident with a person, vehicle or cattle in charge of a person, with intent to escape civil or criminal liability fails to stop his vehicle, give his name and address and, where any person has been injured, offer assistance, is guilty of**
> **(a) an indictable offence and is liable to imprisonment for two years, or**
> **(b) an offence punishable on summary conviction.**

It is obviously in the public interest that anyone who operates a motor vehicle that is involved in an accident should stop, tender assistance if necessary, and identify himself. Few offences arouse such indignation as the hit-and-run offence.

C-3

On July 17, 1943, Robitaille was driving a car from Montreal to Quebec City. At Ancien Lorette, he passed several bicyclists, striking one of them. The evidence showed that Robitaille did not realize that he had caused an accident until later at Quebec City when he heard the news of the accident and the description of the car. He was charged with leaving the scene of an accident. He was acquitted by a judge of the Sessions of the Peace.

> (a) Why was Robitaille acquitted?
> (b) Why is knowledge of the accident essential?

Impaired Driving

> **234.   Every one who, while his ability to drive a motor vehicle is impaired by alcohol or a drug, drives a motor vehicle or has the care or control of a motor vehicle, whether it is in motion or not, is guilty of an indictable offence or an offence punishable on summary conviction and is liable**
> **(a) for a first offence, to a fine of not more than five hundred dollars and not less than fifty dollars or to imprisonment for three months or to both;**

(b) for a second offence, to imprisonment for not more than three months and not less than fourteen days; and
(c) for each subsequent offence, to imprisonment for not more than one year and not less than three months.

Obviously a driver who has too much to drink is a danger to the public. Formerly there were separate offences of driving while intoxicated and a lesser offence of impaired driving. Much time was spent in attempting to distinguish between those who were intoxicated and those who were only impaired. Now the offence of driving while intoxicated has been abolished and the single offence of impaired driving remains which includes all those who would have fallen into either category. The judge can reflect the seriousness of the impairment in the penalty. It will be observed as well that the impairment is a crime whether caused by alcohol or drugs. The section not only creates the offence of impaired driving but also the offence of having care or control of a motor vehicle whether in motion or not.

C-4

On January 18, 1969, about 1:30 p.m., Hollahan was driving an automobile in Halifax and ran into the rear of another vehicle which was stopped and waiting for a light to change. Two police officers arrived, Hollahan was arrested and charged with impaired driving. At the trial, the two police officers testified that when they arrived at the scene, Hollahan smelled of liquor, his eyes were glassy, his speech was thick and slow, and he staggered while walking to the police cruiser. The accused Hollahan said that he had been suffering from the flu and earlier in the day had taken Contac-C pills at 10:15 a.m. At lunch he had a club sandwich, coffee and two beers. He then began to shake and shiver and decided to go home. He took another Contac-C pill and drove towards home when he was involved in the accident. He was convicted in Magistrate's Court. On appeal to the County Court, the conviction was affirmed.

(a) Why was Hollahan convicted?
(b) Does it make any difference that the condition was produced partly by drugs and partly by alcohol?

C-5

King went to his dentist to have two teeth pulled. He was given an injection of sodium pentathol. Earlier he had signed a card which contained a warning against driving after receiving the injection. After regaining consciousness the nurse warned him against driving. King said that he heard no such warning nor did he recall signing any form. He drove his car and lost consciousness, running into the rear of a parked vehicle. King was charged and convicted by a Provincial Judge of driving a motor vehicle while his ability to do so was impaired by a drug. The case was appealed ultimately to the Supreme Court of Canada, which reversed the conviction, holding that there must be a conscious act proceeding from the free will to bring about the condition prohibited by section 234.

(a) What makes this case different from the preceding case?
(b) Why was King acquitted?

C-6

In the early morning of October 6, 1963, at Herbert District, Saskatchewan, the accused, Saunders, was found in an automobile in a ditch beside the road. He was asleep behind the wheel. The key was in the ignition switch and the ignition was turned off. The motor was not running but was capable of running. The automobile could not be moved under its own power and had to be towed out. The accused was in an impaired condition and was charged with the care or control of a motor vehicle while his ability to drive was impaired. He was acquitted by the magistrate on the ground that the vehicle was not at the time a motor vehicle since it was incapable of moving. The case ultimately went to the Supreme Court of Canada which reversed the magistrate's finding.

(a) Why was Saunders charged with "care or control while impaired"?
(b) Why was Saunders convicted by the Supreme Court of Canada?
(c) When would an apparent motor vehicle not be a motor vehicle?

Failure to Provide Breath Sample

235. (1) Where a peace officer on reasonable and probable grounds believes that a person is committing, or at any time within the preceding two hours has committed, an offence under section 234, he may, by demand made to that person forthwith or as soon as practicable, require him to provide then or as soon thereafter as is practicable a sample of his breath suitable to enable an analysis to be made in order to determine the proportion, if any, of alcohol in his blood, and to accompany the peace officer for the purpose of enabling such a sample to be taken.

(2) Every one who, without reasonable excuse, fails or refuses to comply with a demand made to him by a peace officer under subsection (1) is guilty of an offence punishable on summary conviction and is liable to a fine of not less than fifty dollars and not more than one thousand dollars or to imprisonment for not more than six months, or both.

One of the ways in which evidence can be obtained to show the amount of alcohol a driver has consumed is by testing his blood, urine, or breath. For many years the tests were administered only if the subject consented. Many argued that the tests should be compulsory. In 1969, Parliament added this section to the Criminal Code making breath tests compulsory under the circumstances outlined in the section. The results of the tests are admissible as evidence of impairment (section 234) or of an offence under section 236 (see page 73). Since the test is compulsory, refusal to take the test will constitute an offence unless the demand is not justified or unless there is some reasonable excuse for refusing.

C-7

At Summerside, Prince Edward Island, a police officer requested Rushton to provide a sample of his breath. Rushton did blow into the breathalyzer, but only a mere puff from his mouth and not from his lungs. The puff of air was not sufficient for the test. The accused was asked again and again he blew a mere puff. This procedure was repeated a total of five times. In no instance was the puff sufficient for the test. He was charged with failing to provide a breath sample. Rushton was acquitted by the magistrate. On appeal by the Crown, the acquittal was reversed and Rushton was convicted by a judge of the Supreme Court of Prince Edward Island.

> (a) Why do you think Rushton was acquitted by the Magistrate?
> (b) Why do you think he was convicted by the Supreme Court?

C-8

A police officer demanded that Johnson provide a breath sample. Johnson refused on the ground that his ability to drive a motor vehicle was not impaired. Although the police officer had reasonable and probable grounds to think that Johnson had committed the offence of impaired driving, it was subsequently shown that Johnson was not impaired. Johnson was then charged with refusing, without reasonable excuse, to provide a breath sample. The magistrate held that the fact that Johnson was not actually impaired was a reasonable excuse for refusing to provide the breath sample. This ruling was reversed by the Supreme Court of Ontario.

> (a) Do you think that Johnson's reason for refusing the test was a reasonable excuse?
> (b) Why did the Supreme Court of Ontario reverse the ruling of the magistrate?

C-9

Brownridge was arrested for impaired driving and taken to the police station where he was requested to submit to a breath test. He then asked for an opportunity to speak to his lawyer but was refused the opportunity. As a result, Brownridge refused to give the breath sample. Two hours later, Brownridge, then having spoken to his lawyer, offered to give a breath sample and the offer was refused. Brownridge was charged with failing, without reasonable excuse, to provide a breath sample. Brownridge defended on the ground that his excuse was reasonable since the Bill of Rights guarantees to a person who has been arrested or detained the right to retain and instruct counsel without delay. The Provincial Judge who heard the case convicted Brownridge. The case was ultimately appealed to the Supreme Court of Canada which reversed the conviction. Three judges of the Supreme Court of Canada dissented, holding that the section requires immediate compliance and that counsel can be instructed after the section is complied with. The majority of the Court (6) held that a *bona fide* request to retain a lawyer, as guaranteed by the Bill of Rights, was a reasonable excuse.

(a) Why do you think the three judges who dissented felt that the test should be administered immediately?
(b) The majority held that a *bona fide* or honest wish to contact a lawyer first was a reasonable excuse. Why did they limit the excuse this way?

Driving With More Than 80 Mgs. of Alcohol in Blood

236.   Every one who drives a motor vehicle or has the care or control of a motor vehicle, whether it is in motion or not, having consumed alcohol in such a quantity that the proportion thereof in his blood exceeds 80 milligrams of alcohol in 100 millilitres of blood is guilty of an offence punishable on summary conviction and is liable to a fine of not less than fifty dollars and not more than one thousand dollars or to imprisonment for not more than six months, or both.

In response to the increasing problem of the drinking driver, section 236 was also added to the Criminal Code in 1969. While the elimination of the distinction between intoxication and impairment had simplified matters somewhat, the question of impairment is frequently a matter of dispute. The tolerance of people to alcohol varies, and unfortunately too many drivers feel that they can drink substantial amounts without impairing their ability to drive. The above section makes it an offence simply to drive, or have care or control of a motor vehicle while the alcohol in the bloodstream exceeds the prohibited level.

The amount of alcohol in the bloodstream is usually ascertained by testing a person's breath in a breathalyzer machine.

The number of milligrams of alcohol per 100 millilitres of blood in the bloodstream produced by a drink (a 12 oz. bottle of beer, or 1½ oz. of whisky, gin, etc.) varies with the weight of the drinker. Also the body gradually uses or eliminates the alcohol consumed and therefore the mg. level slowly descends, unless of course more alcohol is consumed.

As a result, no simple statement can be made as to how many drinks will produce the 80 mg. level. However, the following examples may be helpful.

- A 185-lb. person who has four drinks in one hour will have, at the end of that hour, 75 mgs. of alcohol per 100 millilitres of blood in the bloodstream. Six drinks would have produced a level of 120 mgs.
- A 160-lb. person who has four drinks in one hour will have, at the end of the hour, a count of 90 mgs. Six drinks would have produced a count of approximately 143 mgs.
- A 120-lb. person who has four drinks in one hour will have, at the end of the hour, a count of 125 mgs. Six drinks would have produced a count of 195 mgs. Three drinks would have produced a count of 90 mgs.

CASES FOR DISCUSSION

1. Roberts borrowed his father's car to go to the library. While there he met several friends and offered them a ride in the car. While driving around Roberts failed to notice a stop sign and proceeded through an intersection. A police officer in a car nearby signalled him to stop. Roberts was concerned that he was supposed to be at the library and not cruising around in his father's car and did not stop, hoping to get away. However, the police car gave chase. The speeds of the vehicles increased and reached a speed of 75 miles per hour in the city. Roberts passed through several more stop signs and finally, unable to stop for a red light at an intersection, collided with a truck crossing his path. Everyone in the Roberts' car was seriously injured.

> (a) Will Roberts be charged with a criminal offence?
> (b) Of which offence do you think he is guilty?

2. Matthews' fellow employees organized a party for him on the occasion of his retirement from the company. Matthews was a non-drinker but was persuaded "to have a few" on this special occasion. After the party broke up, Matthews proceeded to drive home and in the course of doing so failed to notice a car stopping ahead of him and collided with it. The investigating police officer found that Matthews' speech was slurred, that he staggered when he walked, his eyes were glassy, and he smelled of alcohol. Matthews explained that he had no idea that what he had to drink would affect him in this way.

> (a) Is Matthews guilty of impaired driving? Why or why not?
> (b) Would your answer be different if Matthews had been assured that his drink was only a fruit punch?

3.   Chartrand returns home late one night and as he attempts to turn his car into his driveway, his car slips on the ice and collides with a parked car belonging to his neighbour causing about $300.00 worth of damage. It is 4 a.m. and his neighbour's house is in darkness. Chartrand decides not to wake the neighbour or call the police but writes a note giving his name, address, and telephone number and assuming responsibility for the accident and puts it under the windshield wiper of his neighbour's car. He then goes to bed. At 6 o'clock that morning the neighbour finds his damaged car. Chartrand's note has blown away. The neighbour calls the police, who check the cars in the neighbourhood and find Chartrand's damaged car. The paint rubbed off the neighbour's car matches the paint on Chartrand's car. Chartrand is charged with leaving the scene contrary to section 233 of the Criminal Code.

(a) Is he guilty?
(b) Of what significance is the note?

4.   Fennimore was driving home late one evening when his car left the road and struck a tree. The police were called and arrived in a few minutes. Fennimore received a number of cuts and bruises in the accident and was bleeding from a facial cut when the police arrived. He smelled strongly of alcohol and staggered when he walked. The investigating officer asked Fennimore to go to the police station to give a sample of his breath. Fennimore refused saying he wished to go to the hospital to be examined. Fennimore was taken to the hospital where he was treated for superficial injuries and released. He then proceeded to the police station and offered to provide the breath sample. Since it was now four hours since the accident happened, the police declined the offer. Fennimore was charged with failure to provide a sample of his breath contrary to section 235 of the Criminal Code.

(a) Did the police officer have the right to demand the breath sample?
(b) Was Fennimore guilty of the charge of failure to provide the sample?

PART EIGHT
PARTIES TO AN OFFENCE

Obviously the person or persons who actually commit a criminal act are guilty of an offence. However, criminal responsibility will also fall on those who attempt crimes and for some reason fail to achieve their purpose. Guilt will also follow those who play less obvious roles in a crime, either actual or intended.

Parties to an Offence

> **21.   (1) Every one is a party to an offence who**
> **(a) actually commits it,**
> **(b) does or omits to do anything for the purpose of aiding any person to commit it, or**
> **(c) abets any person in committing it.**
> **(2) Where two or more persons form an intention in common to carry out an unlawful purpose and to assist each other therein and any one of them, in carrying out the common purpose, commits an offence, each of them who knew or ought to have known that the commission of the offence would be a probable consequence of carrying out the common purpose is a party to that offence.**

The effect of subsection (1) of this section in general terms is to make anyone who helps another commit an offence a party to it. However, the person who helps must intend to assist the commission of the offence. Example:

A night watchman who deliberately leaves a door open to facilitate a break-in is himself a party to the offence of break and entry. A night watchman who carelessly leaves a door open, but without any intention of facilitating a break-in, will not be guilty of the offence.

Where two or more form an intention to carry out some unlawful purpose, subsection (2) broadens the scope of involvement to foreseeable and probable consequences of the initial unlawful purpose. Example:

Samson and Belanger agree to rob a bank. In the course of the robbery Belanger shoots and wounds a guard. Samson should have known that this second crime was a probable consequence of carrying out the common purpose, i.e., the robbery. Samson is not only guilty of the robbery but will be guilty of the wounding charge as well as Belanger.

A person who is a party to an offence under this section is liable to the same penalty as the person who actually committed the crime.

C-1

Salajko was present when fifteen young men raped a girl in a field. The girl was able to identify only three of the people present, the accused and two others. The other two were convicted of rape but the girl admitted that Salajko did not have intercourse with her and the only evidence against Salajko was that he stood by, passively acquiescing in what was going on. The prosecution argued that he was a party to the offence in that he aided and abetted the others. The jury convicted Salajko. On appeal to the Court of Appeal the conviction was set aside.

> (a) What do you think the jury considered aiding and abetting on the part of Salajko?
> (b) Why did the Appeal Court set aside the conviction?

C-2

The accused Kulbacki was the owner of a car and had permitted his six-teen-year-old girlfriend to drive the car. He was sitting with her in the front seat and did nothing as she drove over 90 miles per hour on an unimproved municipal highway. Kulbacki was charged with dangerous driving on the grounds that he aided and abetted the commission of the offence. He was convicted by the magistrate who heard the case. An appeal to the Manitoba Court of Appeal was dismissed.

> (a) Why was Kulbacki convicted?
> (b) Would any passenger be guilty because he failed to stop the driver?
> (c) Is everyone who allows another to drive a party to an offence committed by the driver?
> (d) Contrast this case with the preceding case.

C-3

Walker was the driver of a get-away car after a robbery. Several miles from the scene of the robbery a police car began to chase the car. In the course of the chase one of the occupants of the car fired a gun at a police officer and wounded him. Walker was charged with attempted murder. The trial judge instructed the jury that they must be satisfied beyond a reasonable doubt that Walker had formed a common intention with the others of shooting someone in the pursuing car before the jury could convict. On appeal the Quebec Court of Appeal held that the instruction given to the jury by the trial judge was wrong and ordered a new trial.

> (a) What should the trial judge have told the jury? (See section 21(2) of the Criminal Code.)
> (b) What common purpose was there at the time the shot was fired?

Counselling

422.   Except where otherwise expressly provided by law, the following provisions apply in respect of persons who counsel, procure or incite other persons to commit offences, namely,
> **(a) every one who counsels, procures or incites another person to commit an indictable offence is, if the offence is not committed, guilty of an indictable offence and is liable**

to the same punishment to which a person who attempts to commit that offence is liable; and

(b) every one who counsels, procures or incites another person to commit an offence punishable on summary conviction is, if the offence is not committed, guilty of an offence punishable on summary conviction.

22. (1) Where a person counsels or procures another person to be a party to an offence and that other person is afterwards a party to that offence, the person who counselled or procured is a party to that offence, notwithstanding that the offence was committed in a way different from that which was counselled or procured.

(2) Every one who counsels or procures another person to be a party to an offence is a party to every offence that the other commits in consequence of the counselling or procuring that the person who counselled or procured knew or ought to have known was likely to be committed in consequence of the counselling or procuring.

Section 422 makes it a crime to counsel (i.e., instruct or advise) or incite (urge or stimulate to action) a person to be a party to an offence. The section also makes it a crime to procure (i.e., get or obtain) another person to be a party to an offence. This latter term is sometimes heard in connection with prostitution. One who arranges to obtain a girl for the purpose of prostitution is said to be a procurer.

Section 22 enlarges the responsibility of those who procure or counsel to include

(a) offences committed in a different way and

(b) other offences committed in consequence of the offence counselled if they should have been foreseen as likely consequences of the first offence.

The offence of counselling, procuring or inciting is complete when those acts take place and it is no defence that the contemplated crime never takes place. There is, however, a difference in the penalty if the offence does not take place. Section 22 makes the person who counsels or procures a party to the offence and he is therefore liable to the same penalty as the person who commits the offence. If the contemplated offence does not take place, section 422 provides that the penalty is the same as for an attempt (see below).

C-4

The accused company published a weekly newspaper distributed to the Vancouver area. The issue published in March 1969 contained a two-page article dealing with the growth and cultivation of marihuana. The article contained a large picture of a marihuana plant and detailed instructions as to how to plant and cultivate marihuana. The article contained at the beginning and at the end the exhortation "Plant Your Seeds". A copy of the paper was sold to Miss Y. and as a result, the company was charged with counselling the commission of an indictable offence, namely the cultivation of marihuana. Miss Y. testified that she was not influenced by the article but was only amused. Georgia Straight Publishing Limited was convicted by the magistrate and appealed to the British Columbia Court of Appeal which dismissed the appeal holding that the offence was committed when the paper was sold to Miss Y. and that it was not necessary that she actually be influenced by the article.

(a) Many newspapers carry stories about drugs. Why did this article constitute counselling?

Accessory After the Fact

23. **(1) An accessory after the fact to an offence is one who, knowing that a person has been a party to the offence, receives, comforts or assists him for the purpose of enabling him to escape.**

(2) No married person whose spouse has been a party to an offence is an accessory after the fact to that offence by receiving, comforting or assisting the spouse for the purpose of enabling the spouse to escape.

(3) No married woman whose husband has been a party to an offence is an accessory after the fact to that offence by receiving, comforting or assisting in his presence and by his authority any other person who has been a party to that offence for the purpose of enabling her husband or that other person to escape.

The plain purpose of this section is to make it a crime for anyone to assist another person who has committed a crime to escape detection or capture. Section 421 (see below) provides liability to the same penalties for those who are accessories after the fact as for those who attempt the offence.

C-5

On May 22, 1875, Ralph Finlay was killed by Smith. Shortly after the killing, Smith, who was a hired man at the family farm, told Mrs. Finlay that he had killed her husband and asked her to keep quiet and give him time to get into bed. She complied, waited a few minutes, and then called both the accused Smith and another person in the house and told them that she was afraid something had happened to her husband. Smith was convicted of murder. The Ontario Court of Appeal held that the actions of Mrs. Finlay made her an accessory after the fact.

(a) What did Mrs. Finlay do that made her an accessory after the fact?

C-6

On September 23, 1948, a police constable was murdered in Montreal. Douglas Perreault was later found guilty of the crime. On the night the murder was committed, the accused Young and others left Montreal heading for Sheenboro, Ontario, about 250 miles away. Just before arriving at Sheenboro, Young met a car driven by Perreault. Young told Perreault that the Montreal police had his (Perreault's) name and the licence number of his car. He offered to hide Perreault at a camp in the woods. Perreault declined but did not proceed to Montreal. He was later apprehended. Young was charged with being an accessory after the fact to murder. He was convicted and his appeal to the Quebec Court of Appeal was dismissed.

> (a) What did Young do which made him an accessory after the fact?

Attempts

> **24.   (1) Every one who, having an intent to commit an offence, does or omits to do anything for the purpose of carrying out his intention is guilty of an attempt to commit the offence whether or not it was possible under the circumstances to commit the offence.**
>
> **(2) The question whether an act or omission by a person who has an intent to commit an offence is or is not mere preparation to commit the offence, and too remote to constitute an attempt to commit the offence, is a question of law.**
>
> **421.   Except where otherwise expressly provided by law, the following provisions apply in respect of persons who attempt to commit or are accessories after the fact to the commission of offences, namely,**
>
> > **(a) every one who attempts to commit or is an accessory after the fact to the commission of an indictable offence for which, upon conviction, an accused is liable to be sentenced to death or to imprisonment for life, is guilty of an indictable offence and is liable to imprisonment for fourteen years;**
> >
> > **(b) every one who attempts to commit or is an accessory after the fact to the commission of an indictable offence for which, upon conviction, an accused is liable to imprisonment for fourteen years or less, is guilty of an indictable offence and is liable to imprisonment for a term that is one-half of the longest term to which a person who is guilty of that offence is liable; and**
> >
> > **(c) every one who attempts to commit or is an accessory after the fact to the commission of an offence punishable on summary conviction is guilty of an offence punishable on summary conviction.**

The offender who attempts an offence and fails is almost as much a danger to the community (perhaps more in some cases) as the offender who succeeds in committing the offence. It is obvious, therefore, that even the attempt to commit a crime must be classified as a crime. The law does not classify a mere guilty intention or even preparation as a crime. The difficulty frequently lies in distinguishing mere preparation from an attempt.

Preparation consists in devising or arranging the means or measures for the commission of the offence; the attempt is the direct movement toward commission after the preparations are made. Putting the matter another way, if one can say with certainty that the crime would have been committed had there not been an interruption, an attempt has taken place.

Section 24, subsection (2) makes this issue a matter of law which thereby assigns the issue to the trial judge, even though the whole case is tried by a jury. The trial judge, in his instructions to the jury, will instruct them as a matter of law where preparation ceases and an attempt begins. The penalties outlined in section 421 are less than those prescribed for the successful commission of the offence itself.

C-7

Three men agreed to rob the Royal Bank on Renfrew Street in Vancouver. They obtained revolvers and ammunition and drove toward the bank. When they were about a block away they saw a police car in front of the bank and drove away. The Supreme Court of Canada held that the action of the three constituted the taking of a necessary step toward the completion of the offence and as a result, the three were guilty of attempted robbery.

(a) Was the formation of the intention enough to constitute an attempt?

(b) At what point did they take the necessary steps?

C-8

Olhauser, on August 20, 1969, went to the Calgary Centre Branch of the Canadian Imperial Bank of Commerce, identified himself as Donald Webb, gave a fictitious address, and opened an account. He was given a book of cheques bearing the number of the account. He falsely stated that he had an account at the main branch of the Canadian Imperial Bank of Commerce at Edmonton and signed an order to transfer the balance of the Edmonton account to his new account. On the same day, Olhauser opened an account at the Fourth Street West branch of the Royal Bank of Canada under the name of Gordon Stack and received a book of cheques bearing the account number. On August 21, Olhauser returned to the Calgary Centre Branch and gave the teller a deposit slip and a cheque for $700.00. The cheque was drawn on the Royal Bank signed "Gordon Stack" and endorsed by "Don Webb". On August 22, Olhauser returned to the Calgary Centre Branch and the police, having been alerted by a teller who had telephoned the Royal Bank branch about the Gordon Stack cheque, arrested Olhauser. He was charged with attempting to obtain money from the Canadian Imperial Bank of Commerce by means of a false pretense. The defence was that these were acts of preparation and that Olhauser still had not attempted to get any money. He was convicted by the trial judge and appealed to the Alberta Supreme Court. The appeal was dismissed.

(a) What was the purpose of the various steps taken by Olhauser?
(b) Why did Olhauser's actions constitute an attempt?

Conspiracy

423. (1) Except where otherwise expressly provided by law, the following provisions apply in respect of conspiracy, namely,
(a) every one who conspires with any one to commit murder or to cause another person to be murdered, whether in Canada or not, is guilty of an indictable offence and is liable to imprisonment for fourteen years;
(b) every one who conspires with any one to prosecute a person for an alleged offence, knowing that he did not commit that offence, is guilty of an indictable offence and is liable
(i) to imprisonment for ten years, if the alleged offence is one for which, upon conviction, that person would be liable to be sentenced to death or to imprisonment for life or for fourteen years, or
(ii) to imprisonment for five years, if the alleged offence is one for which, upon conviction, that person would be liable to imprisonment for less than fourteen years;
(c) every one who conspires with any one to induce, by false pretences, false representations or other fraudulent means, a woman to commit adultery or fornication, is guilty of an indictable offence and is liable to imprisonment for two years; and
(d) every one who conspires with any one to commit an indictable offence not provided for in paragraph (a), (b) or (c) is guilty of an indictable offence and is liable to the same punishment as that to which an accused who is guilty of that offence would, upon conviction, be liable.
(2) Every one who conspires with any one
(a) to effect an unlawful purpose, or
(b) to effect a lawful purpose by unlawful means,
is guilty of an indictable offence and is liable to imprisonment for two years.

A conspiracy is an agreement between two or more to do an unlawful act or to do a lawful act by unlawful means. There must be a genuine common design to do something unlawful. If one of two persons merely pretends to agree without any intention of carrying out the agreement into effect, there cannot be a conviction for conspiracy. The essence of the offence is the agreement and it is not necessary to show that any act was done in furtherance of the conspiracy. It is only rarely possible to prove the agreement by direct evidence; ordinarily a conspiracy is established entirely by showing the actions of the parties. Example:

> Three men sitting in a car near a bank are arrested. Each is found to be carrying a revolver and a stocking mask. Each has a pair of gloves in his pocket despite the fact that it is July. One of the men has a sketch of the floor plan of the bank in his pocket.
>   Do these facts prove any agreement among the three? If so, what?

Section 423, subsections (a), (b) and (c), deal with specific kinds of conspiracy. Section 423(d) deals with a conspiracy to commit any indictable offence not covered in the prior three subsections. Section 423, subsection (2) is stated in wider terms and includes a conspiracy to commit a summary conviction offence or a conspiracy to effect a lawful purpose by criminal means.

C-9

O'Brien approached Tulley and suggested that Tulley assist him to kidnap a certain Mrs. P. Tulley agreed. Later Tulley communicated with Mrs. P. and told her of O'Brien's intention. O'Brien was arrested and charged with conspiracy to kidnap. It was Tulley's evidence that he only pretended to carry out the agreement. O'Brien was convicted but his conviction was reversed by the Supreme Court of Canada.

   (a) Is there an agreement if a party only pretends agreement?
   (b) Why did the Supreme Court of Canada reverse the conviction?

C-10

Caron and Funnell appeared before a Provincial Judge charged that they did on or about November 7, 1969, at the City of Toronto, conspire to commit robbery. Funnell pleaded guilty and was sentenced to five years in the penitentiary. Caron pleaded not guilty. A preliminary hearing was held and the case proceeded to trial. Caron was found not guilty. As a result of this verdict, Funnell appealed his conviction to the Ontario Court of Appeal. Funnell was acquitted by the Ontario Court of Appeal.

   (a) If two persons are alleged to be conspirators, how can only one be guilty?
   (b) If three were charged, could one be found not guilty and two convicted?
   (c) Why did the Ontario Court of Appeal acquit Funnell?

CASES FOR DISCUSSION

1.   Foster and Brooks decide to rob the local Brinks office. As they plan the robbery, it becomes apparent that if they are to succeed they must have inside help. They approach Dolan, an employee of Brinks, and sound him out. Dolan is heavily in debt and receptive to the plan. The three agree to share equally. Dolan furnishes the timetables of Brinks from which it can be ascertained when the most money will be on the premises, the number of guards, etc. Dolan also furnishes detailed floor plans and agrees to open a door at a prearranged time to admit Brooks and Foster. Dolan is to play no further part in the matter so that his involvement will not be detected.

   The robbery begins according to plan; Foster and Brooks, masked and armed, enter through the door opened by Dolan. All goes according to plan but as Brooks and Foster are filling sacks with money, a guard attempts to reach for an alarm button. Brooks panics and shoots the guard, killing him. They then take the sacks and flee. Brooks and Foster are apprehended two days later and Dolan's part in the affair is exposed.

   (a) Brooks is guilty of murder. Is Foster also guilty of murder? Why or why not?
   (b) Is Dolan guilty of robbery? Why or why not?
   (c) Is Dolan also guilty of murder? Why or why not?

2.   Fricker, an undercover police officer, becomes friendly with a group of people long suspected by the police of criminal activities. One of the group, Masters, asks Fricker if he would like to make a little money. Fricker replies that he would. Masters then outlines to Fricker a plan to rob a bank. The participants are to be Masters and Fricker and others that they will recruit later. When he finishes telling him of the plan, Masters says, "What do you say? Are you in?" Fricker replies, "Okay, count me in." Masters is arrested and charged with conspiracy to commit robbery.

   (a) Is he guilty of conspiracy? Why or why not?

3.   Walters, an employee of Thunderball Motors, is fired. Unable to find another job because of his poor work record, he conceives a plan to kidnap Penelope Bunker, the twelve-year-old daughter of P. T. Bunker, owner of Thunderball Motors, and hold her for ransom. He takes up a look-out and learns the timetable of the Bunker household, specifically when Penelope goes to and returns from school. He photographs her through a telephoto lens to become familiar with her appearance. He then rents an old farmhouse where he intends to hold the girl when he kidnaps her and equips it with food. A neighbour of the Bunkers who has seen Walters in the area several times calls the police; the police search Walters' farmhouse and find the timetable prepared by Walters, a photograph of Penelope and a gun. Walters is arrested and charged with attempted kidnapping.

   (a) Is Walters guilty of attempting kidnapping or has his conduct constituted only preparation? Discuss.

III

DEFENCES

A person accused of crime is presumed to be innocent until his guilt is established beyond a reasonable doubt. A criminal case commences with the Crown (prosecution) calling such evidence as it has available to show the accused is guilty. At the conclusion of the Crown's case, the defence may choose to call no evidence on the ground that the prosecution has not proved its case, or the defence may, if it wishes, call the accused himself to testify and/or such other witnesses as he wishes.

GENERAL DENIAL

In most cases that go to trial, the defence evidence is simply a denial of the Crown evidence relating to the whole charge or one of its elements. For example,

(1) Atkinson is charged with the murder of Buchanan in a barroom brawl. Crown witnesses testify that they saw Atkinson pull a gun and fire at Buchanan. Atkinson testifies that while he was present in the room he was not the one who fired the gun at Buchanan and calls several witnesses who were sitting with him to confirm his testimony.
(2) Atkinson is charged with the murder of Buchanan. Atkinson testifies that while he caused the death of Buchanan it was accidental.

In some instances, the defence may be of a more specific nature and these will be dealt with separately. With one exception (double jeopardy), it is not necessary for an accused, in answer to the charge, to say what his defence is. It is sufficient to say "not guilty"; nothing more is required. With the exception of insanity and double jeopardy, it is not necessary for the accused to prove his defence or satisfy a judge or jury that it is true. If the defence raises a reasonable doubt as to guilt in the minds of the jury, or the judge if the case is tried without a jury, then the accused is entitled to be acquitted. An accused is not restricted to one defence but it is entitled to raise as many defences as the nature of the case and the facts will allow.

SPECIFIC DEFENCES

Insanity

Section 16 of the Criminal Code states:

(1) No person shall be convicted of an offence in respect of an act or omission on his part while he was insane.

(2) For the purposes of this section a person is insane when he is in a state of natural imbecility or has disease of the mind to an extent that renders him incapable of appreciating the nature and quality of an act or omission or of knowing that an act or omission is wrong.

(3) A person who has specific delusions, but is in other respects sane, shall not be acquitted on the ground of insanity unless the delusions caused him to believe in the existence of a state of things that, if it existed, would have justified or excused his act or omission.

(4) Every one shall, until the contrary is proved, be presumed to be and to have been sane.

The concept of insanity in this section is based on the statements of English judges in *McNaghten's Case,* 1843. This definition does not reflect modern psychiatric thinking but no acceptable amendment to the section has been produced. Governed by this section, Canadian courts have not accepted irresistible impulse as a species of insanity. The onus of establishing insanity is on the accused. He is not obliged to prove insanity beyond a reasonable doubt; he must show that it is probable. An accused who is found not guilty by reason of insanity is not released but is kept in custody until the appropriate authorities are satisfied that he is sane. Frequently the custody is permanent.

C-1

The accused was charged with rape. Expert medical testimony established that the accused was a psychopath and the act was committed as a result of this condition and was a product of an uncontrollable urge. The accused was unable to learn from experience or control his impulses. He had a maladjusted personality in that his conduct often brought him into conflict with society. His actions were unplanned and guided by whims. The accused was convicted.

    (a) What is a psychopath?
    (b) Do you agree with the verdict? Why or why not?
    (c) Do you think the legal definition of "insanity" should be enlarged?

Non-insane Automatism

The term automatism denotes unconscious involuntary conduct. If the automatism is produced by a disease of the mind, the matter must be considered as a defence of insanity. However, automatism can be produced by factors other than insanity, for example, a blow to the head, sleepwalking, a physical disease. If a person is acquitted on the grounds of non-insane automatism, he is released, unlike the person who is found not guilty by reason of insanity.

C-2

Quick was charged with assaulting Green. There was no question that Quick had struck Green several times. The evidence, however, was that Quick was a diabetic and that when Quick struck Green he was suffering from hypoglycaemia (a condition where there is too much insulin in the bloodstream), which can cause violence and unconsciousness in the sufferer. The English Court of Appeal held that the accused was entitled to be acquitted.

  (a) Why was the accused acquitted?
  (b) An accused in a case of this type who is acquitted is released. Should he be? Compare those acquitted by reason of automatism with those found not guilty by reason of insanity.

The Incapacity of Children

> **12.   No person shall be convicted of an offence in respect of an act or omission on his part while he was under the age of seven years.**
> **13.   No person shall be convicted of an offence in respect of an act or omission on his part while he was seven years of age or more, but under the age of fourteen years, unless he was competent to know the nature and consequences of his conduct and to appreciate that it was wrong.**

The law presumes that children under the age of seven are not capable of appreciating the nature and consequences of their acts to such a degree to render them criminally responsible. A child between seven and fourteen may possess sufficient understanding but the prosecution must prove his competence.

Intoxication

Generally, intoxication either by alcohol or drugs is not a defence to a criminal charge. There are, however, two exceptional situations.

In some instances, an accused may, by consuming drugs or alcohol, bring on a disease of the mind to the extent that he is temporarily insane within the meaning of insanity as defined earlier. In other instances, where the offence is one in which a specific intention is an essential element, evidence of intoxication may show that the accused was not capable of forming the necessary intent. For example:

> Albert is charged with the murder of Buchan by shooting him. The evidence is that Albert was in an advanced state of intoxication. The evidence may make it questionable as to whether or not Albert intended to kill Buchan or cause him bodily harm which he knew was likely to cause death. If a reasonable doubt exists, Albert will be acquitted of murder but convicted of manslaughter. Manslaughter requires only a general intent.

Mistake of Fact

In those crimes which require a guilty mind or *mens rea,* a mistake of fact will constitute a defence if (1) the mistake is reasonable and (2) there would have been no crime if the facts had been as the accused thought them to be. For example, a person who on reasonable grounds, but mistakenly, believes his spouse to be dead does not commit bigamy in going through a second marriage.

While a mistake of fact can be a defence to a criminal charge, the same cannot be said of a mistake of law. As a result, it is often said ignorance of the law is no excuse. One exception to this rule regarding a mistake of law concerns the crime of theft. An erroneous belief caused by a mistake of law that one has a right to goods is a defence to a charge of theft.

> ### C-3
> The accused brought into Canada a quantity of gems, rings, vases and jewellery boxes as household goods under his wife's name. He was charged with a violation of the Customs Act. His defence was that he believed he was entitled to bring the goods into Canada as household goods. He was convicted by a Provincial Court Judge and the conviction was upheld by the Ontario Court of Appeal.
>
> > (a) Why was the accused convicted?
> > (b) Should his mistake have any effect on the sentence?

Self Defence

> **34. (1) Every one who is unlawfully assaulted without having provoked the assault is justified in repelling force by force if the force he uses is not intended to cause death or grievous bodily harm and is no more than is necessary to enable him to defend himself.**
>
> **(2) Every one who is unlawfully assaulted and who causes**

death or grievous bodily harm in repelling the assault is justified if

> **(a) he causes it under reasonable apprehension of death or grievous bodily harm from the violence with which the assault was originally made or with which the assailant pursues his purposes, and**
>
> **(b) he believes, on reasonable and probable grounds, that he cannot otherwise preserve himself from death or grievous bodily harm.**

35.   Every one who has without justification assaulted another but did not commence the assault with intent to cause death or grievous bodily harm, or has without justification provoked an assault upon himself by another, may justify the use of force subsequent to the assault if

> **(a) he uses the force**
>
>> **(i) under reasonable apprehension of death or grievous bodily harm from the violence of the person whom he has assaulted or provoked, and**
>>
>> **(ii) in the belief, on reasonable and probable grounds, that it is necessary in order to preserve himself from death or grievous bodily harm;**
>
> **(b) he did not, at any time before the necessity of preserving himself from death or grievous bodily harm arose, endeavour to cause death or grievous bodily harm; and**
>
> **(c) he declined further conflict and quitted or retreated from it as far as it was feasible to do so before the necessity of preserving himself from death or grievous bodily harm arose.**

Section 34 justifies the use of reasonable force when a person is defending himself against an unprovoked attack. For example:

> O'Neill, while walking home, is approached by Rogers, who says, "I'm going to teach you who is boss" and hits O'Neill. O'Neill is entitled to use reasonable force to defend himself. See section 34(1). He may even intend to cause grievous bodily harm or to kill if he reasonably believes he will suffer grievous bodily harm or death and there appears to be no other way to save himself. See section 34(2).

Section 35 deals with the situation where one person has commenced an assault, but without intent to cause serious harm, and is then obliged to defend himself against a counter-attack which threatens death or grievous bodily harm. For example:

> O'Neill decides to pick a fight with Green and punches him in the chest. O'Neill intends only a schoolboy fight and does not intend serious harm. Green counter-attacks with such fury and force that O'Neill fears either

death or grievous bodily harm. O'Neill must first try to quit the fight but if he cannot, he is entitled to use reasonable force to defend himself.

> **37.   (1) Everyone is justified in using force to defend himself or any one under his protection from assault, if he uses no more force than is necessary to prevent the assault or the repetition of it.**
>
> **(2) Nothing in this section shall be deemed to justify the wilful infliction of any hurt or mischief that is excessive, having regard to the nature of the assault that the force used was intended to prevent.**

Section 37 differs from sections 34 and 35 in that those sections deal with defence from assaults or counter-assaults. Section 37 deals with the *prevention* of an assault from taking place either on one's self or on anyone within one's protection. As in the previous sections, the governing principle is *reasonable force*. Sections 38 and 39 entitle one to use reasonable force to defend one's goods.

C-4

C, a fourteen-year-old boy, lived with his father, his mother having died when he was six. The boy and father lived alone and the relationship was not a happy one. One night in 1964 the father returned to the house, armed himself with a 30-30 rifle, and advanced up the stairs saying, "I'm going to kill that —— —— little ——." The boy loaded his 22 rifle, and as his father advanced up the stairs, the boy fired five shots which struck his father. Two of the shots were fatal. A Juvenile Court held that the amount of force used was not reasonable and the boy was convicted. On appeal, a Saskatchewan Supreme Court judge reversed the decision, holding that the degree of force cannot be measured exactly and that the test is whether the accused used more force than he on *reasonable grounds believed necessary.*

(a) What would be the difference between the force actually necessary and the force the boy reasonably believed to be necessary?

(b) Should the test of self-defence be based on the degree of force actually necessary or what is reasonably *believed* to be necessary? Give your reasons.

Defence of Dwelling

> **40.   Every one who is in peaceable possession of a dwelling-house, and every one lawfully assisting him or acting under his authority, is justified in using as much force as is necessary to**

prevent any person from forcibly breaking into or forcibly entering the dwelling-house without lawful authority.
41. (1) Every one who is in peaceable possession of a dwelling-
house or real property and every one lawfully assisting him or
acting under his authority is justified in using force to prevent any
person from trespassing on the dwelling-house or real property,
or to remove a trespasser therefrom, if he uses no more force
than is necessary.

These two sections extend the principle of self-defence to the home and
entitle a person to defend against entry and eject the trespasser if he has entered. The principle of reasonable force, however, continues to be the primary
consideration.

C-5

On December 23, 1969, at Whitehorse, Yukon Territory, after midnight
two men entered the home of Taylor, who was in bed at the time. Taylor
asked them to leave but they continued to advance toward him. He picked
up a rifle and fired at the floor. The bullet struck one of the men in the leg.
Taylor had had several break-ins during the past month. Taylor was
charged with the unlawful use of a firearm and acquitted in Magistrate's
Court.

    (a) Why was Taylor acquitted?
    (b) In this case was the firing of the rifle necessary or should
         another method of defence have been tried first? Give
         your reasons.
    (c) According to section 41(1) of the Criminal Code, is one
         entitled to shoot trespassers? Explain.

Alibi

Alibi is the Latin word for "elsewhere". In legal terms "alibi" means the defence in which it is claimed that the accused was elsewhere at the time of the
commission of the offence. This type of defence is simply a specific example of
a general denial. It is generally considered, however, that an alibi defence
should be raised as soon as possible, i.e., in a statement to the police shortly
after arrest or in a statement made at the preliminary hearing. An alibi defence
that is raised for the first time at trial when there is no opportunity by the
prosecution to investigate it may be regarded with suspicion.

Double Jeopardy

It is a principle of our law that no one should be punished more than once for
the same offence. It is also a principle of our law that one should not be

charged again for an offence for which he has already been found not guilty or pardoned. This type of plea must be made specifically giving the details of the prior conviction, acquittal or pardon. This rule applies only where the charge is for the *same* offence.

Further, this rule deals with separate proceedings. On occasion a person may be tried for an offence and for some reason the trial is defective.

> For example, inadmissible evidence is given at the trial, faulty instructions are given to the jury, etc.

The Court of Appeal may order a new trial. The second trial is a part of the same proceeding on the original charge and the double jeopardy rule may not be invoked.

Compulsion

Compulsion may be a defence to a criminal charge and can arise as a result of threats or by force of circumstances. The Criminal Code deals specifically with compulsion by threats.

> **17.   A person who commits an offence under compulsion by threats of immediate death or grievous bodily harm from a person who is present when the offence is committed is excused for committing the offence if he believes that the threats will be carried out and if he is not a party to a conspiracy or association whereby he is subject to compulsion, but this section does not apply where the offence that is committed is treason, murder, piracy, attempted murder, assisting in rape, forcible abduction, robbery, causing bodily harm or arson.**

Clearly, a person who at gunpoint is forced to help a thief should not be guilty of an offence. However, the principle has its limits in that one cannot commit extremely serious acts no matter what the compulsion.

Compulsion by force of circumstances or necessity, as it is sometimes termed, has not been defined by the Criminal Code and remains a common law defence. Such cases are extremely rare. It appears that if one commits an act that would otherwise be a crime to avoid some much greater evil, he will have a good defence. For example:

> While strolling on a wharf in a harbour, Adams sees a man drowning in the water. Adams snatches a rope and life jacket from a yacht moored nearby and throws them to the drowning man. The taking of the rope or life preserver is not considered an offence.

C-6

In 1884 the English yacht Mignonette foundered on the high seas 1600 miles from the Cape of Good Hope. Four members of the crew, Dudley, Stevens, Brooks, and Parker, a boy of about seventeen years of age, set off in an open boat. They had no food or water except two one-pound tins of turnips. For the first three days they lived on the turnips. On the fourth day they caught a small turtle and occasionally they caught some rain water.

On the eighteenth day, Dudley and Stevens spoke to Brooks suggesting that one of the four should be sacrificed to save the rest. Brooks disagreed. Parker was not consulted. They were 1000 miles from land and by the twentieth day no ships had appeared. Parker was very weak, lying at the bottom of the boat, when Dudley, with Stevens' concurrence, killed Parker by putting a knife in his throat. For the next four days the three fed upon the boy's body and blood. On the fourth day they were picked up by a passing ship. Dudley and Stevens were returned to England and charged with murder. The jury found that (1) if the three had not eaten the boy's body they probably would not have survived, (2) that Parker was likely to have died before them, (3) at the time of the killing there was no reasonable prospect of rescue, (4) that it appeared probable to the prisoners that unless one was killed all would die. The jury found these facts by way of special verdict but was unable to say whether they constituted murder. The case was sent to a panel of five judges for decision who found the two accused guilty and sentenced them to hang. The five-judge Court held that there was not such necessity as could justify the killing of the boy. The sentence of the Court was not carried out but was later commuted or changed by the Crown to a sentence of six months' imprisonment.

(a) Do you agree with the decision of the Court—the commutation of the sentence?

(b) If the defence of necessity could succeed in these circumstances, how should it be determined who should be the first to be killed?

(c) If the principle of necessity had succeeded, would it permit the survivors to kill again and so on until only one remained?

CASES FOR DISCUSSION

1. Angstrom believes himself to be the Prime Minister of Transylvania. He further believes that his next door neighbour Basset is a member of his government who is plotting to overthrow his government. As Basset passes Angstrom's house one day, Angstrom rushes out the door shouting, "Death to the traitor" and runs his sword through Basset killing him. Angstrom is arrested and charged with non-capital murder. A psychiatrist testifies that Angstrom is insane and suffers delusions.

(a) Is Angstrom guilty of murder? Why or why not?

2. Harris, while playing football, is struck on the head and suffers a concussion but continues to play. Shortly thereafter the referee calls a penalty

against Harris and Harris strikes the referee. Harris is taken from the game to the locker room where the trainer notices a lump on Harris' head. Harris is taken to the hospital and held for observation. The next morning Harris has no recollection of the game.

(a) Is Harris guilty of assaulting the referee? Why or why not?

3.   Carson's infant son falls from his high chair injuring himself and begins to bleed from the mouth. Carson takes the boy to his car and drives directly to the hospital where the boy is given emergency treatment. At the hospital Carson encounters a police officer who recalls that a month prior, as a result of an impaired driving conviction, Carson was prohibited from driving for a period of six months. Carson is charged with driving a car while prohibited from driving.

(a) Does Carson have a defence to this charge? Why or why not?

4.   Bernice, a nervous housewife, is married to Archie, a salesman who is obliged to travel a great deal in the course of his work. Archie completes his travelling assignment early one week and returns home late Thursday night although he is not expected until Friday. Archie has forgotten his key and rather than awaken the household, he attempts to enter through the kitchen window. Bernice, who is not asleep at the time, hears the window being raised. In a state of fear she takes her husband's shotgun from its case. As her husband walks up the unlit stairway to the second floor towards the bedroom, Bernice shoots him, wounding him seriously. Bernice is charged with attempted murder.

(a) Is she guilty of this offence? Why or why not?

IV
INVESTIGATION, ARREST, AND BAIL

THE POLICE

A committee appointed by the federal government to study criminal justice stated that the criminal law "is only a literary exercise unless there be police to enforce it".

There is in Canada a national police force—the RCMP; two provincial police forces—the Ontario Provincial Police and the Quebec Provincial Police; and approximately 750 municipal police forces. Exclusive of civilian personnel, the RCMP numbers approximately 10,000, the OPP 4,000, the QPP 4,000 and the various municipal forces 25,000. The municipal police forces range in size from Metropolitan Montreal—5,500—to rural township forces of one man.

The various police forces have assumed responsibility in various areas as a matter of practice, but all come within the definition of peace officers in the Criminal Code and exercise the powers of that office. For example, even though the RCMP has assumed the primary responsibility for enforcing the Narcotic Control Act, any other police officer may arrest for an offence against that Act.

Police Functions

The primary functions of the police are to:
   (1) prevent crime;
   (2) detect crime and apprehend offenders;
   (3) to maintain order in the community in accord with the law.

Despite the popular picture of policemen devoting the bulk of their time to the detection of crime and the apprehension of criminals, police officers spend more of their time doing other things; the control of traffic and the investigation of accidents, the control of crowds, settling family quarrels before they become violent, finding the lost, and simply assisting those in trouble are all a large part of modern police work.

In 1972, the Metropolitan Toronto police force handled 41 murder cases but investigated 50,000 automobile accidents. The same force investigated 1,594 robberies that year but also dealt with 10,508 missing persons cases, locating 96% of the missing.

In this chapter some of the functions of the police relating to the suppression of crime will be dealt with, e.g., investigation, arrest, etc. These functions do not occur in any necessary sequence. In some cases the police activity commences with an arrest and an investigation follows.

> Example: The police are called to the house of Thompson. On arrival they find his wife dead, having been shot in the head. Thompson's gun is found with one cartridge expended. Thompson is the only person in the house. He is arrested immediately. The investigation, fingerprints, ballistics, statements, etc., will follow.

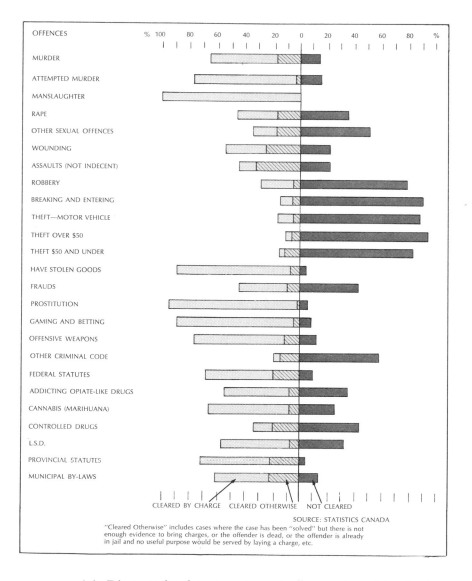

SOURCE: STATISTICS CANADA

"Cleared Otherwise" includes cases where the case has been "solved" but there is not enough evidence to bring charges, or the offender is dead, or the offender is already in jail and no useful purpose would be served by laying a charge, etc.

(a) Discuss why the percentage of offences cleared by the laying of charges varies so much with the type of offence. Consider contacting your local police force for assistance in this discussion.

In other cases when a crime is reported, months of careful and painstaking investigation will lead to an arrest and even in those cases, part of the investigation may take place after the arrest.

Police Questioning

The police are entitled to question anyone in the furtherance of an investigation. Those questioned usually fall into two classes: (1) those who can provide information and who may be witnesses and (2) the suspect himself from whom an incriminating statement is sought. Generally, no one is legally obliged to answer the questions of the police but there are some exceptions created by statute. For example, the driver of a car involved in an accident is obliged to give a report; a person entering Canada is obliged to state to a Customs Officer whether or not he has any goods to declare, etc.

Most citizens, however, feel it a duty to do all they can to co-operate with the police. The person who himself is the object of the investigation may choose to remain silent for reasons of his own.

Questioning the Accused

In the course of investigation, the person who is ultimately charged may be questioned like anyone else. Once the police reach the point where they feel there are reasonable grounds to believe a certain person has committed an offence, he should be *cautioned,* i.e., told (1) that he may be charged, (2) the nature of the offence, (3) that he need not say anything, and (4) that whatever he does say will be taken down in writing and may be given in evidence at his trial.

A statement made by an accused either before or after the caution will be admissible against him at trial only if it is given voluntarily, in the sense that it was not obtained from him by fear, of prejudice or hope of advantage exercised or held out by a person in authority.

The fact that a caution is given does not necessarily mean that any statement given thereafter is voluntary. Nor does the absence of a caution necessarily indicate that a statement given without one is involuntary. A judge in ruling whether a statement is admissible or not will look to the presence or absence of a caution as one factor only in determining whether or not the statement was given voluntary.

C-1
The accused, LeBlanc, was arrested and charged with two offences of theft over $50.00. The accused was shown certain goods alleged to have been stolen and was told that no bail arrangements would be made until a statement was obtained. As a result, the accused gave a statement admitting guilt. The British Columbia Court of Appeal set aside the conviction on the ground that the statement was not admissible against the accused.

(a) Why was LeBlanc's statement not admissible?
(b) If LeBlanc had been cautioned after he was told that no bail arrangements would be made, would the statement then be admissible?

ARREST

A person is arrested when he is deprived of his liberty. This is usually accomplished by an officer taking charge of a person either physically or by words and telling the person he is under arrest.

Without a Warrant

A police officer may arrest without a warrant: (1) a person whom he finds committing a criminal offence of any description, (2) a person who *has* committed an indictable offence, (3) a person whom he *believes* on reasonable grounds has committed or is about to commit an indictable offence.

C-2

In Kitimat, B.C., a police officer saw McKibbon driving in a somewhat erratic manner. The officer pursued the accused to a place where both cars stopped. In asking for the driver's licence, the officer noticed the smell of alcohol on the accused's breath and noted also that when the driver got out of the car he was unsteady on his feet. The officer demanded that the accused take a breathalyzer test. The accused ran, pursued by the police officer, who seized him and said that he was under arrest. A struggle ensued. A subsequent breathalyzer test indicated the accused was not impaired and no charge of impaired driving was laid but he was charged with assault with intent to resist arrest. The defence was that the arrest was not lawful. The Provincial Judge acquitted the accused of assaulting with intent to resist arrest and convicted him only of common assault. The British Columbia Court of Appeal reversed the Provincial Judge's decision and convicted the accused of assault with intent to resist arrest.

(a) What do you think was the basis of the acquittal by the Provincial Judge?
(b) Why was the result changed by the British Columbia Court of Appeal?

The Criminal Code, however, provides that in the case of the least serious offences, unless the public interest requires it, the accused should not be arrested but should be issued an appearance notice by a police officer requiring him to appear in court at a specified time. In many instances involving less serious offences, a police officer will neither arrest nor issue an appearance notice but will simply swear an information (a brief statement as to the nature of the case) before a Justice of the Peace who will issue a summons which requires the accused to appear in court. The principal difference between the summons and the appearance notice is that the Justice of the Peace makes the decision as to whether the summons should be issued.

With a Warrant

If, however, it is necessary in the public interest, a Justice of the Peace may issue a warrant for the arrest of an accused. Any police officer to whom the warrant is directed may then arrest the accused.

Duty of Arresting Officer

It is the duty of the officer who makes an arrest, either with or without a warrant, to tell the person arrested why he is being arrested, if at all possible. If the arrest is made with a warrant, the officer should have the warrant with him and produce it if requested to do so.

Arrest on Suspicion or for Questioning

There is no right to arrest a person except as indicated above. Police officers may request a person to come to the police station for the purposes of answering questions but if the person does not wish to do so, the police officer must let him go his way or make an arrest for a specific offence based on reasonable probable grounds.

Fingerprinting and Photographing

Anyone charged with an indictable offence may be photographed, fingerprinted, weighed, measured, pursuant to the Identification of Criminals Act.

SEARCH

Search of Premises

The search of one's premises involves a gross invasion of liberty and privacy and may be performed only under limited circumstances.

With a Warrant

The Criminal Code authorizes a Justice of the Peace to issue a warrant to a police officer giving him the power to search premises and seize articles found. Before issuing the warrant, the Justice of the Peace must be satisfied by a sworn statement that there are good grounds for believing that the premises contain anything used or to be used in the commission of an offence or evidence of an offence.

As an Incident of Arrest

There is also power in the police, once an arrest has taken place, to search the premises under the control of the person arrested, as well as his automobile or other means of travel.

Search of the Person

Ordinarily a person may be searched only after he has been arrested. The police may search for weapons and for articles that may be evidence of the offence charged. With the exception of some special statutory provisions, the right to search the person exists only as an incident of arrest, e.g., special rights of search of premises under the Narcotic Control Act extend to a search of persons on the premises.

C-3

Several years ago at Hamilton, the RCMP had reasonable grounds to believe that Brezack had committed or was about to commit an offence against the Opium and Narcotic Drug Act (now the Narcotic Control Act). Several constables seized Brezack on the street, arresting him. Constable M caught Brezack by the throat to prevent him from swallowing anything he might have in his mouth. After a considerable struggle, which involved Brezack biting Constable M's fingers a number of times, Constable M finally got his fingers in Brezack's mouth to satisfy himself that Brezack was not concealing any drugs. Brezack was charged with assaulting an officer in the execution of his duties. Brezack's defence was that Constable M had no right to search his mouth and that Constable M in fact had assaulted Brezack. The Ontario Court of Appeal held the search of Brezack's mouth was lawful.

    (a) On what basis do you think the Ontario Court of Appeal found the search to be lawful? Give reasons for your agreement or disagreement with the results.

C-4

The accused was believed to have been involved in a holdup in which shots were exchanged. Eighteen months later he was arrested on another matter. The police then obtained a search warrant to search the accused's body for bullets which might link him with the first offence. The search was to be conducted by a doctor. The surgery required was more than superficial. The Quebec Court of Queen's Bench declared the search warrant invalid.

    (a) Why did the Quebec Court of Queen's Bench set aside the search warrant?

    (b) What change in the above facts might have made the proposed search legal? Discuss.

Illegally Obtained Evidence

Generally speaking, evidence that is relevant to a charge is admissible against an accused even if it is obtained illegally. The fact that evidence is obtained by an illegal search or other illegal methods does not affect its admissibility at trial or its value. However, illegal searches or other illegal methods may expose the police to prosecution or civil action. There are, however, two exceptions to the general rule regarding illegally obtained evidence: (a) confessions—as previously discussed, the law treats statements given by an accused to a person in authority in a special way. Unless such a statement is given voluntarily it will not be admissible; (b) private communications—as a result of the growth in the use of different methods of electronic eavesdropping, the Criminal Code was amended in 1974 to prohibit the interception of private conversations by electromagnetic, mechanical, accoustic or other devices. The prohibition does not apply if one party to the conversation consents to the interception or if the interception is authorized by a judge's order. A judge's order may authorize interceptions for a period of thirty days and may be renewed for further thirty day periods. Nor does the prohibition apply in cases involving national security, if the interception is authorized by the Solicitor General of Canada. Conversations that have been intercepted contrary to the Criminal Code are not admissible against the parties to the conversation unless one of the parties consents.

> Example: The police bugged the phone of Earp and intercepted conversations wherein Mellon called Earp and admitted that he murdered Bean. To make this interception legal and the evidence admissible, the police, prior to the interception, should have obtained either a court order or the consent of either Earp or Mellon.

However, even if the interception was illegal, the conversation can be used as evidence if either Earp or Mellon will consent to its use, even though the interception has already taken place.

INTERIM RELEASE

Prior to 1971, a person who was arrested would be released pending trial only if bail could be arranged. Most often the bail took the form of cash or property posted as security. In minor cases the bail might simply be recognizance, i.e., a promise signed by the accused either alone or with others to pay a certain sum of money if he failed to appear for trial.

In 1971, Parliament amended the Criminal Code and substantially changed the law with respect to the release of arrested persons while awaiting trial. In less serious offences, the officer who made the arrest or the officer in charge of the police station may release an arrested person unless it is against the public interest or unless there are reasonable grounds to believe that the accused will not appear in court. However, when an arrested person is kept in custody he must be brought before a Justice of the Peace, magistrate or Provincial Judge within twenty-four hours or, if none is available, as soon as possible.

The Criminal Code further provides that when the person in custody is taken before a Justice of the Peace and pleads not guilty to the charges, unless the prosecution shows cause to the contrary, the accused shall be released on his undertaking (promise) to appear for trial.

If the prosecution does show cause why the accused should not be released on his simple undertaking to appear for trial, then resort may be had to other alternatives. The Justice of the Peace may release the accused (a) on his undertaking to appear with certain conditions imposed, for example, that he report to a police station once a week; (b) on the accused entering into a recognizance. The recognizance may be with or without sureties, co-signers, and with or without conditions and (c) if the accused does not live in the province where he is charged or lives more than 100 miles away from the place where he is charged, the Justice may also order the posting of a deposit (cash).

In some cases the person charged may not be released pending trial. The Justice may order that the accused be detained in custody if the prosecution can show (1) that it is necessary to ensure his attendance in Court or (2) that it is necessary in the public interest or for the protection and safety of the public.

C-5
The accused had a record commencing in 1956 and continuing until 1969 when he was sentenced to four years for break and entry. He was paroled in July 1970. While on parole he was arrested and charged with three robberies. He applied for bail, which was refused.

> (a) On what basis was bail refused?
> (b) Do you agree with the decision? Why or why not?

RIGHT TO COUNSEL

The Canadian Bill of Rights expressly recognizes (a) the right of a person arrested to retain a lawyer without delay and (b) the right of a person to a fair hearing in accordance with the principles of fundamental justice for the determination of his rights and obligations.

The police have no right while holding a person in custody to prevent him from communicating with a lawyer.

Legal Aid

In the past, however, those who were unable to afford a lawyer found this right to retain a lawyer to be an empty one. Beginning in the 1950s, the various Provincial Bar Associations instituted voluntary legal aid plans whereby defence counsel were provided to accused persons who could not afford them. While these voluntary plans provided a great deal of help to many people, the plans were not totally satisfactory and could not satisfy the need. In 1967, Ontario adopted a comprehensive legal aid plan. Under this plan a person without sufficient funds and in need of defence counsel other than for trivial matters may apply to the legal aid officer for his area. It is then determined whether he can pay part or none of the legal expense. A certificate may then be issued to the applicant to cover the full or part of his legal expenses. This certificate enables the applicant to retain a lawyer of his choice. The legal aid plan then pays the lawyer 75% of the ordinary charge.

The above process, of course, takes time. To fill the gap, legal aid also provides duty counsel who are immediately accessible to those in Court or in custody who give advice of a general nature.

Since 1967, all the provinces except Prince Edward Island have adopted similar legal aid plans. In Prince Edward Island, however, the Attorney General's department in certain cases appoints counsel for the accused. The various legal aid plans are financed by the province in which they operate and in 1972 the federal government agreed to share the cost of these plans. There is presently no reason why anyone accused of a serious crime in Canada may not take advantage of his right to retain a lawyer.

C-6

Steeves was arrested and charged with leaving the scene of an accident contrary to the Criminal Code. He was not allowed to contact a lawyer without delay, although later he was able to retain a lawyer for the trial. During the interview that took place before Steeves was able to retain a lawyer, he revealed the name of one Edwards who was later called by the prosecution as a witness. The magistrate who heard the case dismissed the charge because of the contravention of the Bill of Rights. The Nova Scotia Court of Appeal, however, reversed the magistrate's decision, pointing out that Steeves had been represented by counsel at the trial before the magistrate, even though he had been denied the right to obtain a lawyer immediately. The Appeal Court further pointed out that this breach of the Bill of Rights did not of itself entitle the accused to an acquittal and that there might be other remedies available for the breach of the Bill of Rights, for example, a civil suit for damages.

  (a) Do you agree with this decision? Why?
  (b) If the accused had been deprived of his right to counsel at trial, would the decision have been different? Explain.

DISCUSSION

1. In some countries evidence that is obtained illegally is not admissible against the accused.
    (a) Is this the case in Canadian law?
    (b) Should the fact that evidence is obtained illegally prevent the truth from being shown?
2. The Canadian Criminal Code now prohibits electronic eavesdropping, bugging telephones, etc., without either a court order or the consent of one of the parties to the conversation to be overheard.
    (a) Do you agree that the police should be restricted in this way?
    (b) Should citizens be exposed to unrestricted electronic eavesdropping? Discuss.
3. A police officer may arrest, without a warrant, a person whom he be-

lieves on reasonable grounds has committed an indictable offence.

(a) Is this right of arrest too broad, too narrow? Discuss.

(b) Should those arrested mistakenly be compensated? Why or why not?

4.   Some jurisdictions have "stop and frisk" laws which confer upon the police wide powers to search persons. These powers are not dependent upon arrest.

(a) Are you in favour of such a law for Canada? Discuss.

CASES FOR DISCUSSION

1.   Shannon was the driver of a car carying several passengers. The passengers were suspected of theft by the police. The car was stopped and Shannon allowed the officer to see the inside of the car and trunk. Nothing was found. The officer then asked Shannon to go to the police station. When Shannon refused, the officer informed him that he was taking the car to the police station. A disturbance followed. The New Brunswick Court of Appeal held that the officer had no right to seize the car.

(a) What was the basis of this ruling?

(b) What additional facts would have made the seizure lawful?

2.   Kaspar was arrested on board an Air Canada D.C. 8 at the Toronto International Airport and was found to have in his possession a plastic explosive device that was not detected by the search equipment before boarding. Kaspar was taken into custody and charged with contravening section 76(2) (endangering safety of an aircraft) of the Criminal Code. Kaspar identified himself as a student at a Toronto University. He was twenty-four years old and resided in an eastern European country. The next morning Kaspar was arraigned in Provincial Court.

(a) Should Kaspar be released on bail or detained in custody?

(b) If he is to be released on bail should there be conditions? Discuss.

3.   Mallon was a mechanic in a garage that remained open twenty-four hours a day. He always parked his own car in an alley which separated the rear of the garage from a warehouse. One night Mallon, having finished work, proceeded to his car dressed in coveralls carrying his tool box. At the same time, officer Ross had received a radio call that the alarm system at the warehouse had been triggered and was instructed to investigate a possible break-in. Ross drove his police cruiser into the alley behind the warehouse and his headlights illuminated Mallon putting a box in the trunk of his car. Ross called out, "Stop, you are under arrest." Mallon, blinded by the headlights, was unable to see either Ross or the police car. Fearing that he was about to be robbed, Mallon ran. Ross jumped from the police cruiser and tackled Mallon, throwing him to the ground and breaking Mallon's arm. The true facts are discovered and Mallon claims damages. The police department answers that Mallon was attempting to escape a lawful arrest.

(a) Was the arrest lawful?

(b) What is the critical point in the determination of this issue?

V

TRIAL

The court and method of trial vary in criminal cases and depend upon the nature of the charge and, in many cases, the choice of the accused. At common law, crimes were divided into treasons, felonies, and misdemeanours. Treason included crimes against the security of the state; felonies included most of the other serious crimes and usually involved the death penalty; and misdemeanours included the less serious offences. The Criminal Code, however, eliminated those distinctions and crimes are now divides into two classes:

(1) offences punishable on summary conviction,
(2) indictable offences.

SUMMARY CONVICTION

Summary conviction cases are the less serious offences. Following arrest or summons to appear in court, the accused person is tried by a magistrate without a jury. These cases are heard in Magistrate's Court with a minimum of delay, hence the term summary trial. Examples of summary conviction cases are: creating a disturbance, selling a firearm to a person under sixteen and many of the offences committed in the operation of a motor vehicle.

INDICTABLE OFFENCES

Generally speaking, indictable offences include all the serious offences in the Criminal Code. The term "indictable" is derived from "indictment" which was the written accusation presented by the grand jury. As a result of being indicted, an accused in earlier times was then always tried by a jury. The grand jury has now been abolished in many of the provinces and an increasing percentage of cases are tried by a judge without a jury. Criminal jury trials, however, still being with an indictment, i.e., a written accusation. The term "indictable", therefore, continues to have meaning in that it includes the serious cases which are at least capable of being tried by a judge and jury.

Indictable offences must be further classified to determine the available trial procedure.

Class A: the least serious indictable offences, such as theft under $200 or conducting an illegal lottery, are within the absolute jurisdiction of a Magistrate (in many provinces called Provincial Judge). Even in these cases, however, the Magistrate, if it appears proper, may direct that the charge proceed by way of indictment.

Class B: the most serious cases such as treason and murder must be tried in the Supreme Court of the province with a jury. The names in the various provinces vary—Supreme Court, Court of Queen's Bench, etc. In Alberta, however, an accused may consent to be tried by a Supreme Court Judge without a jury.

Class C: for all other indictable offences (which is the largest group) the accused may elect to be tried either (1) by a Magistrate (Provincial Judge); (2) by a judge alone. In Ontario, New Brunswick, Nova Scotia, and Prince Edward Island, this means a judge of the County or District Court; (3) by a judge and jury. In Ontario, New Brunswick, and British Columbia, trial by judge and jury can mean trial by a Supreme Court Judge and jury or a County or District Court Judge and jury. In all of the other provinces, trial by judge and jury means a Judge of the Supreme Court of the province and a jury.

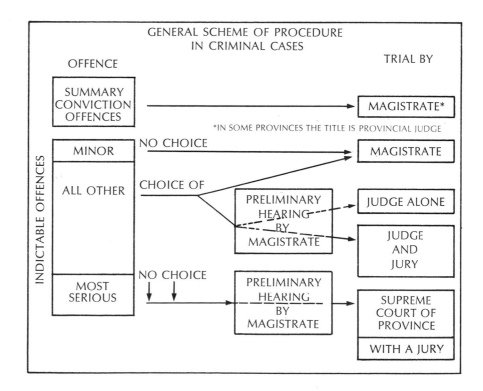

In the case of indictable offences, an accused appears first before a Justice of the Peace or magistrate. Justices of the Peace have extremely limited powers to hear cases and in most instances will simply deal with the issue of bail and adjourn the matter to the appropriate court. If the offence is an indictable offence within Class A, an accused is read the charge and asked for his plea. If the plea is not guilty, a date is set for trial and the trial proceeded with.

If the offence is within Class B, the charge is read to the accused and a date is set for a preliminary hearing. If the preliminary hearing shows a case of probable guilt, the accused is committed for trial before a Supreme Court Judge and jury.

If the offence is within Class C, the magistrate reads the charge and then proceeds to ask the accused how he elects to be tried. If the accused elects to be tried by the magistrate, a plea is then asked for and if it is not guilty, a date is set for trial. If the accused elects to be tried by a judge alone or a judge and jury, the magistrate must conduct a preliminary hearing. At the preliminary hearing, witnesses are called by the prosecution and cross-examined by counsel for the accused. The magistrate must then decide if a case of probable guilt has been established. If not, the accused is discharged. If it is, he is committed for trial. The preliminary hearing is not a trial and dismissal of a charge at this stage is not a bar to further proceedings.

C-1
Smith was charged with wounding and also with having a weapon dangerous to the public peace. He was brought to court on the wounding charge and elected trial before a magistrate and the trial was proceeded with. As soon as the wounding trial was completed, the trial on the dangerous weapons charge was proceeded with and by inadvertence the accused was not asked for his election on that charge and was convicted. The Ontario Court of Appeal set aside the conviction on the second charge.

> (a) Why was the election so important that its omission led to the conviction being set aside?

A Plea of Guilty

An accused may not wish to be tried and may be prepared to plead guilty. Even a guilty plea, however, must be entered before a court that has jurisdiction. In the case of a summary conviction offence or Class A of the indictable offences, the accused, when read the charge, may simply plead guilty. If the charge is within Class C, the accused must first elect how he wishes to be tried. Usually an accused who wishes to plead guilty will elect trial before the magistrate to save time. If he wishes, however, he may elect trial by judge and jury or trial by judge alone and then plead guilty before either one of those courts. In the most serious cases, Class B, a plea can be accepted only by a Supreme Court Judge. If a guilty plea is entered, there is, of course, no necessity for a trial. The courts, however, will usually require the prosecutor to disclose the facts upon which the charge was based. These facts are sometimes related by witnesses or sometimes read from a report by the Crown Attorney. Courts are careful to see that the facts justify the charge and also that the accused person has not pleaded guilty out of ignorance or fear. If a court is not satisfied that a guilty plea is warranted, the guilty plea will be struck out and a plea of not guilty substituted for the accused so that a trial may be held and the issue of guilt or its absence established. Courts are particularly careful in the case of young people who may plead guilty simply to avoid any further difficulty or publicity when in fact they may not be guilty of the offence.

C-2
Brosseau was fifteen years old and had dropped out of school in the second grade. Indicted for capital murder, he pleaded not guilty. The case was adjourned several times and then the charge was reduced to non-capital murder. Brosseau pleaded not guilty to non-capital murder but after a short adjournment he changed his plea and pleaded guilty to non-capital murder. He was then given the mandatory life penalty. The accused was represented by counsel when he entered his guilty plea. The Judge did not enquire as to whether the boy understood the charge and the consequence of the plea. An appeal was launched to the Supreme Court of Alberta and then to the Supreme Court of Canada. Both Appeal Courts dismissed the appeal. The Supreme Court of Canada held that while failure to conduct an inquiry into whether the accused understood the charge and the effect of his plea could be a ground of appeal, in this case there was no duty to conduct such an inquiry.

>   (a) Why was the court under no duty to conduct an inquiry in this case?

NON-JURY TRIALS

Depending on the nature of the charge and the election of the accused, a trial may take place before a magistrate or before a judge alone. In these cases the trial proceeds in the same way. The charge is first read to the accused and he is asked for his plea. If he pleads guilty there is, of course, no trial (see above). If the accused pleads not guilty, the Crown Attorney may or may not make a short opening statement to the court in which he outlines the nature of the case to be proceeded with. In summary conviction cases and other minor matters this is seldom done. The prosecution then calls its witnesses and by questioning adduces their testimony from them. Defence counsel or the accused himself, if he is unrepresented, is entitled to cross-examine each witness. The purpose of the cross-examination may be to bring out other facts from the witness which tend to explain or qualify the testimony already given or to show that the testimony given is unreliable. When the prosecution has called all of its witnesses, the defence may call witnesses and the prosecution may cross-examine. At the conclusion of the defence evidence, the prosecution may call witnesses in reply for the purpose of dealing with any new issues that have been raised in the defence.

At the close of the evidence, both the Crown Attorney and defence counsel are entitled to make a closing speech to the judge in which they sum up their case. The judge may then give the decision forthwith or may delay it for a short time. If the accused is found guilty, he will be sentenced either forthwith or at a later date. If he is found not guilty, he is discharged (except in insanity cases).

The Accused and Spouse as Witnesses

An accused person may testify or not as he wishes, and in no case can he be forced to testify. The prosecution cannot call an accused as a witness. The same rule applies to the spouse of the accused, with some exceptions. In those cases where the spouse or the children are the victims, the spouse of an accused may be called by the prosecution and forced to testify. If the trial takes place before a jury, neither the Crown prosecutor nor the trial judge may comment upon the failure of the accused or his spouse to testify.

JURY TRIALS

As we have seen, in some instances the accused must be tried by a Supreme Court Judge and jury and in other cases he may elect to be tried by a judge and jury. Although in essence a jury trial is the same as a non-jury trial it is somewhat different procedurally.

Jurors

The Criminal Code does not lay down any qualifications for jurors but simply adopts the qualifications in the province where the trial takes place. The Criminal Code has, however, recently been amended to provide that no one should be disqualified as a juror on the grounds of sex, thereby insuring that women may serve as jurors. The provincial qualifications for jurors vary somewhat but in general terms the list of jurors is taken from the municipal voters lists. In some instances this requires that the jurors or spouses be either owners or tenants of property. From these lists, panels of jurors (approximately 100) are selected by a selection board to attend the sittings of the Court.

Grand Jury

In Newfoundland, Nova Scotia, Prince Edward Island, and Ontario, the grand jury still exists. A grand jury is specially selected from the jury lists. The function of the grand jury is to inquire into the indictments presented for trial at that sittings of the court (see Statutes of Clarendon, p. 4). The grand jury does not try the issue of guilt but simply determines if there is enough evidence to place the accused on trial. The fact that this determination has already been made by a magistrate at the preliminary hearing has led many critics to say that the function of the grand jury is a waste of time. Most of the provinces, as well as England, have abolished the grand jury. In those provinces where the grand jury still exists, they must endorse the indictment as a "true bill" before the trial proceeds. If they find there is not sufficient evidence to warrant a trial they endorse the indictment "no bill" and the accused is discharged.

Petit (Petty) Jury

Assuming that a true bill has been returned in those provinces where it is necessary, the indictment is read to the accused and he is asked for his plea. If he pleads not guilty, the next step is the selection of a petit jury. The name "petit" was acquired in early days to distinguish it from the "grand" jury. All of the jurors on the panel are assembled in a court room and the name of each on a separate card is placed in a box and shaken together. The clerk proceeds to draw cards in turn. As each juror comes forward, either prosecution or defence may state that they are "content" with the juror or, on the other hand, he may be challenged either for cause or peremptorily either by the Crown Attorney or by the defence.

A juror may be challenged for cause if there is some valid reason why the juror will not be independent, if he is physically unable to perform his duty, or if he has been convicted of a serious criminal offence.

In addition to challenges for cause, the defence has a number of peremptory challenges, i.e., a juror may be objected to without any reason being given. The number of peremptory challenges varies from four to twenty depending on the seriousness of the offence. The prosecution has four peremptory challenges. Jurors who are successfully challenged for cause or challenged peremptorily, may not serve on the petit jury in the case in which they are challenged but they may serve on other juries at the same sittings. In addition to challenges, the prosecution may ask a juror to stand aside. If a jury has not been selected by the time the last card is drawn, the "stand-asides" are called again. Each juror who successfully passes through the selection process is sworn and takes his seat in the jury box. When twelve have been so selected, the process is complete. (In the Yukon and Northwest Territories the jury is composed of six jurors.)

THE TRIAL

Once the twelve jurors are selected, it is customary for the presiding judge to make a short opening speech outlining to the jurors the nature of their duties. The prosecution then makes a short address describing, in general terms, the nature of the case to be tried so that the jury may better appreciate the evidence as it is called. Once this is done the trial proceeds in the same manner as a non-jury trial—witnesses are called, etc. The pace of the trial, however, is usually somewhat slower since it is important that the jury hear and understand all that is being said. At the conclusion of the evidence both defence and Crown counsel make their closing speeches to the jury. The trial judge then delivers the charge, a speech in which the case is reviewed for the jury. In the charge the judge instructs the jurors as to (1) the general principles applicable to the trial, e.g., the obligation on the Crown to prove the accused guilty beyond a reasonable doubt; (2) defines and explains the law as it pertains to the case being tried; and (3) reviews the facts of the case and relates the facts to the law.

Verdict

The jury then leaves the courtroom in the custody of the court constables to consider its verdict. During the trial, except in unusual circumstances, jurors leave the courtroom for lunch and at the end of the day. Once they retire to consider their verdict, however, they are kept together and are provided with meals and overnight accommodation, if necessary. In order to reach a verdict of either guilty or not guilty, the jury must be unanimous. From their number the jurors elect a foreman whose duty it is to preside over their deliberations and announce their verdict when they reach one. A jury that cannot agree is somtimes called a "hung jury" and reports its disagreement to the trial judge who directs a new trial. A jury's deliberations are secret and even the jurors are prohibited from disclosing to anyone what transpired in the course of their deliberations. When an agreement is reached, the jurors return to the courtroom and the foreman announces the verdict. If the accused is found not guilty he is discharged; if guilty he is sentenced by the judge either at that time or later. The jury takes no part in the sentencing process.

JUVENILE DELINQUENTS ACT

Juvenile offenders are dealt with differently from others. "Juvenile" is defined in the Juvenile Delinquents Act as "anyone under the age of sixteen years". Provision is made, however, for provincial variation. As a result, in Quebec and Manitoba the age has been varied to under eighteen; Alberta—girls under eighteen, boys under sixteen; British Columbia—under seventeen. The Act provides that any breach of the criminal law, provincial statute, or municipal by-law is classified as a delinquency. A juvenile who has committed an offence is brought before the Juvenile Court either by arrest or summons and charged simply as being delinquent. In the case of an indictable offence, however, where the child is over fourteen, the Juvenile Court may order that he be dealt with by indictment in the ordinary courts. In the Juvenile Court the child is dealt with as a person who needs help and supervision. If he is found to be delinquent, the juvenile may be put on probation, fined up to $25.00, be placed in a foster home, committed to the charge of the Children's Aid Society, or committed to an industrial school or juvenile reformatory. A child under twelve, however, may not be committed to an industrial school until an effort has been made to reform the child at his own home, foster home, or in the charge of the Children's Aid Society.

Hearings in Juvenile Court are conducted summarily and in private without publicity.

APPEALS

Indictable Offences

Any person who is convicted of an indictable offence may appeal his conviction or sentence to the Court of Appeal for the province in which the conviction took place. Similarly, the prosecution may appeal an acquittal or a sentence which it considers too low. Appeals are almost always simply a review of the written transcript of the trial. Only in rare instances is fresh evidence called before the Appeal Court.

These general rights of appeal by both the accused and the prosecution are, however, limited to some degree.

Appeal by the Accused

A person who has been sentenced to death has a *right* to appeal on any ground—either on the basis of fact, i.e., the trial court came to a wrong conclusion on the facts, or on a point of law, i.e., at the trial the law was misunderstood or misapplied.

One who has been convicted of any other indictable offence has a right to appeal his conviction only on a point of law. If he wishes to appeal on a question of fact or on a mixed question of fact and law or the sentence, he can do so only with the leave (permission) of the Appeal Court.

Prosecution Appeals

The prosecution has a right to appeal only on a question of law. If the Crown wishes to appeal a sentence, it can do so only with the leave of the Appeal Court. The prosecution may not appeal on a question of fact.

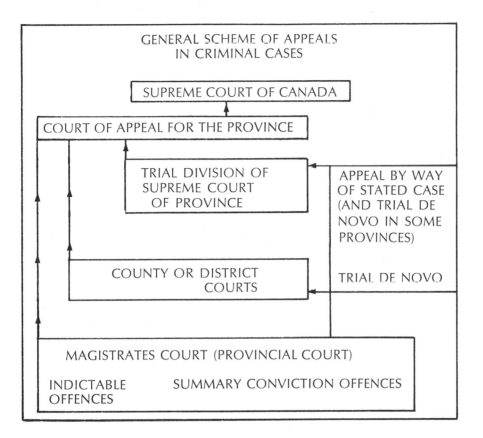

Summary Conviction Offences

This type of offence is tried by a magistrate (or in some cases by a Justice of the Peace). Both the Crown and the accused are entitled to appeal the result. The appeal can be conducted in either one of two ways, trial *de novo* or by way of stated case.

Trial De Novo

An appeal by way of trial *de novo*, as the name suggests, is simply a new trial before a judge of a higher court. Witnesses are called to testify, exhibits are produced, and oral argument is presented. In Newfoundland and Prince Edward Island an appeal is heard before a judge of the Supreme Court, in Quebec before a judge of the Queen's Bench, in all of the other provinces before a judge of the County or District Court. Neither side is restricted to the same evidence that was called in the first trial.

Stated Case

Where the basis of the appeal is a question of law alone, the person appealing may require the magistrate to state the facts of the case and the legal question in writing. The case thus stated is argued before a single judge of the Supreme Court of the province who determines the legal issue and, as a result, whether the magistrate was right or wrong.

The decision reached in either the trial *de novo* or the stated case may be further appealed on a question of law to the Court of Appeal for the province with the leave of that court.

Appeals to the Supreme Court of Canada

It is possible to appeal from the decision of the Court of Appeal of a province to the Supreme Court of Canada. A person who has been sentenced to death may appeal on any ground—law or fact.

In other cases, the right to appeal is somewhat restricted. In indictable offences the Crown or accused have a right to appeal to the Supreme Court of Canada on a question of law in which there has been a dissenting judgment in the Provincial Court of Appeal, i.e., the members of the Provincial Court of Appeal have not been unanimous—one or more have dissented from the majority opinion. Appeals from Provincial Courts of Appeal in which there has been no dissent may be heard only with leave. Summary conviction cases as well may be appealed only with leave.

DISCUSSION

1.   From time to time there is controversy about the worth of the jury trial.
     (a) Should the right to trial by jury be retained or abolished? Discuss.

2.   A jury must be unanimous to reach a verdict. As a result, one juror can cause a mistrial.
     (a) Should eleven out of twelve or some other fraction be sufficient for a verdict? Why or why not?

3.   What considerations could lead an accused to elect
     (a) trial by magistrate
     (b) trial by judge alone
     (c) trial by judge and jury?

VI
SENTENCING

If an accused is found not guilty (except where he is found not guilty by reason of insanity), he is free to go. If, on the other hand, he has pleaded guilty or is found guilty of the offence with which he is charged or of a lesser included offence, the immediate problem is the difficult question of sentence. With few exceptions (murder, importing narcotics, etc.), the law sets no exact penalty or even a minimum penalty. Most of our criminal legislation fixes only maximum penalties. The penalty is therefore left to be determined by the trial judge within the maximum limit. Even in cases tried by juries, the jury determines the issue of guilt and the issue of sentence is determined by the judge.

Consideration of the penalty necessarily involves a consideration of the purposes of the criminal law. It is said that the basic purpose of the criminal law is to protect all members of society, including the offender himself, from seriously harmful and dangerous conduct. There are a number of theories as to how the sentence may best protect society.

RETRIBUTION

Punishment for crime until the nineteenth century tended to be harsh to the point of brutality. It was felt that a person convicted of crime should suffer and thereby *pay* for his crime. In a more enlightened and humane era, the retributive theory has largely disappeared from the criminal sentence. It continues to linger, however, in the case of the most serious and heinous crimes.

Some modern writers have argued that there may be a basis for the retributive theory in limited instances on the grounds that retributive sentences for heinous crimes stifle the urge to private vengeance.

Sir James Stevens, a famous English criminal lawyer, said that the criminal law bears to the instinct of revenge the same relation that the institution of marriage bears to the sexual instinct. Both contain and regulate strong human instincts which, if not given some form of legitimate expression, will find satisfaction otherwise.

DETERRENCE

The deterrent theory of sentencing is based on the proposition that the threat of punishment will deter people from the commission of crime and, therefore, the sentence should be sufficient to make the threat operative. A person who is convicted of crime has already demonstrated that the mere threat of punishment did not restrain him. It is thought that the actual experience of conviction and punishment will sharpen the appreciation of the threat and that the convicted person will be restrained from further crime by the threat of punishment again. In this sense the deterrent quality of the sentence is described as a special deterrent.

To the extent that the penalty imposed restrains others from the commission of the same offence, the deterrent quality is described as a general deterrent.

In its narrowest sense, deterrence suggests that a person, when confronted with the choice of committing a crime or not, weighs the benefit to himself against the threat of punishment and makes a decision. One would think that this process is not a common occurrence. In a wider sense, however, the sentence may deter crime by indirectly restraining criminal conduct. A sentence, by emphasizing community disapproval of an act and branding it as reprehensible, has a moral or educative effect and thereby affects the attitude of the public. A person with a strong attitude conditioned to regard a type of conduct as reprehensible will likely not consider such conduct at all and not even get to the point where he must be restrained by the threat of punishment. Some legal writers believe that one of the most important functions of the criminal law is education or conditioning.

REHABILITATION AND REFORM

The most humane theory of dealing with the convicted person is that he should be rehabilitated and reformed. In most cases, prisoners are ultimately returned to society; even those sentenced to life imprisonment may be paroled. Therefore, if the convicted person, by a process of education and persuasion, can be corrected, i.e., changed to a person who wishes to lead a crime-free life, society will be protected because the danger has been eliminated. A person who is trained and thereby equipped to obtain a job at an attractive wage will not likely be motivated to steal. Similarly, an offender with psychiatric problems who is treated and cured will likely no longer be a danger to society. In the last century the theory of rehabilitation and reform has played a large part in the criminal law. This approach has enjoyed some success and, as the critics are quick to point out, some failures as well. However, the process of reform and rehabilitation, which is often difficult and uncertain, continues to be a most desirable goal.

PREVENTION

Obviously a prisoner does not normally constitute any further danger to society during the very time he is held in custody. To this extent, any sentence of imprisonment involves a preventive quality. In some instances, however, this aspect of sentencing may be the major consideration. A persistent offender who will not be deterred or reformed is likely to receive a sentence which is in large measure preventive. The Criminal Code makes special provision for the habitual criminal and the dangerous sexual offender. If an accused, after being convicted of an indictable offence, is, in a separate hearing, shown to be a habitual criminal, he may be sentenced to an indefinite period of imprisonment. Similarly, a person who is convicted of a serious sexual offence, and who is in a separate hearing found to be a dangerous sexual offender, may be sentenced to an indefinite period of imprisonment. Clearly in these two instances the whole object of the indefinite imprisonment is preventive.

MAN GETS LIFE FOR HEROIN COUNT

TORONTO—A New York City man convicted of trafficking in 25 pounds of Asian heroin worth $4-million on the street was sentenced Monday to life imprisonment.

Judge Janet Boland said there had been no evidence of previous charges or convictions against Ng Yuen Hing, a 37-year-old cook she convicted earlier, but these factors were eclipsed by others. Trafficking in heroin for profit is one of the most serious offences known to the law, and the courts consider it to be a sinister, cold-blooded and ruthless crime, Judge Boland said.

Ng's case marked the first time that the brown, Asian heroin had appeared in Ontario, and there was uncontradicted evidence that Ng had advised an undercover agent in New York City that he was one of four men in control of 25 pounds of heroin in Toronto, Judge Boland said.

She said traffickers must realize that they are subject to the most severe penalty the courts can exact. There was no evidence Ng was an addict.

In view of the fact that Ng had no criminal record, can you account for the severity of the sentence?

It is said that the policy of our law with respect to sentencing is unsatisfactory because the theories just described are largely inconsistent with each other. There is a measure of validity in this criticism. However, it has not been demonstrated that any single approach provides the answer. A variety of approaches is used depending on the type of crime committed and the type of person who committed the crime.

The trial judge who has heard the case will know the details of the offence, but before passing sentence in the more serious cases, he will attempt to learn what he can about the offender—his age, family status, educational background, employment record, previous convictions if any, etc. These details may come directly from the accused or his counsel or may be provided by the Probation Department in a pre-sentence report. Subject to the Criminal Code, the following types of sentence may be imposed:

(a) Death

In Canada, the death penalty is still imposed for one form of murder and the more serious forms of treason and piracy. The sentence is accomplished by hanging. In such a case, when the accused is convicted, the trial judge is obliged to ask the jury whether or not they recommend clemency. Irrespective of the answer, the trial judge is required to pass the sentence of death but the Federal Cabinet may commute the death sentence to one of imprisonment.

(b) Corporal Punishment

Until recently, whipping was a possible punishment for some sex offences and crimes of violence, although it was rarely imposed. On July 15, 1972, all reference to whipping as a punishment was deleted from the Criminal Code.

(c) Imprisonment

For the more serious offences, an accused may be imprisoned. The responsibility for prisons is divided between the federal government and the provinces. The federal government maintains a system of penitentiaries where terms of two years or more are served. If the term is less than two years, the time is served in a provincial prison. The type and quality of provincial prisons vary. In some provinces there is a wide range of institutions; in others there is not. In Ontario, there is a system of local jails (sometimes spelled gaol), one for each county and district where prisoners serving less than three months are held as well as prisoners awaiting trial. Those serving time for more than three months are confined in provincial reformatories. Most police forces have a local lock-up for the purpose of holding prisoners temporarily but prison terms are not served in them.

There are approximately 24,000 persons held in the prisons of Canada. Approximately 8,000 are held in the federal penitentiaries and the balance in the various provincial institutions. With respect to the approximately 16,000 in provincial institutions, it should be remembered that this figure includes many persons who are serving terms that may be as short as a few days. Included as well are some 3,300 juveniles held at training schools.

In Canadian Penitentiaries:

8 out of 10 come from urban areas

7 out of 10 have not progressed beyond grade 8

8 out of 10 have been previously convicted

6 out of 10 were unemployed when arrested

7 out of 10 are serving terms of less than 5 years

4 out of 10 have served previous terms of imprisonment

What general conclusions can you draw from these statistics?

One obvious purpose of the prison is to hold the inmate in custody for the period of his sentence. The other purpose is to prepare the prisoner for return to the community as a law-abiding citizen. In the case of short sentences (10 days, 30 days, etc.), nothing can be done by way of training or education but in the case of longer sentences efforts are made to reform and rehabilitate the prisoner. Prisoners may take technical training in a variety of trades. Opportunities are also available for academic up-grading up to and including university.

Intermittent Terms

Where a sentence of imprisonment does not exceed ninety days, a court may direct the sentence to be served intermittently at such times specified by the court, e.g., on weekends, nights, etc.

Consecutive and Concurrent Terms

If an accused is convicted of more than one offence and receives a sentence of imprisonment for each offence, the terms may be served at the same time (concurrently) or one after the other (consecutively) as the court orders.

Parole

Parole is the release of a prisoner to finish the unexpired portion of his sentence under the supervision and guidance of a parole officer. An inmate of a penitentiary must serve at least nine months of his sentence, but may be released on parole after serving one-third of his sentence or four years, whichever is less. There is a variety of types of parole—full parole lasting months or years, gradual parole so that the offender may adjust to the community before being released, day parole for special training or other rehabilitative reasons. A parolee who breaches the conditions of his parole or who commits another offence may be returned to custody to serve the balance of the term that was outstanding when he was released. In addition to parole, which is handled by the Parole Board, the penitentiary and reformatory authorities may authorize temporary absences for medical, humanitarian, and rehabilitative reasons.

Time Off for Good Behaviour

Prisoners in federal and provincial prisons are credited with remission of one-quarter of the sentence subject to good behaviour. In addition, a prisoner may earn an additional three days a month by industry and application.

C-1

The accused pleaded guilty to robbery before a Judge of the Sessions of the Peace in Quebec and received a sentence of fifteen months' imprisonment. The evidence showed that the accused was armed at the time he committed the robbery. The accused was a young man but had three previous convictions for break and entry and a conviction for dangerous driving. The robbery itself was committed within six months after the accused had been released on parole as a result of his last conviction for break and entry. The Quebec Court of Appeal increased the sentence to seven years.

(a) Why did the Quebec Court of Appeal increase the sentence?

C-2

The accused was involved in a bank robbery on December 7, 1970. She was charged and released on bail. On December 13, 1970, she visited a co-accused in jail and was found to be carrying a concealed weapon and was charged with that offence. She was convicted of both offences at London, Ontario, and received seven years for the robbery and six months for carrying the concealed weapon, the sentences to be served concurrently. The Ontario Court of Appeal varied the sentence by making the terms consecutive.

(a) Why did the Ontario Court of Appeal vary the sentence?

(d) Suspended Sentence and Probation

When no minimum penalty is provided, a court may suspend the passing of sentence and release the accused upon conditions prescribed in a probation order. The maximum period is three years. The probation order must contain conditions that the accused will keep the peace and be of good behaviour and will appear in court when called. The court may add extra terms requiring the accused to report to and be supervised by a probation officer, abstain from alcohol, attempt to find a job, etc., and, generally speaking, any other term that the court considers desirable to secure his good conduct and the protection of the community.

Suspended sentences are commonly misunderstood. A suspended sentence does not necessarily mean that the sentence will be no more than a period of probation. If an accused at any time during the probationary period breaches the terms, he may then be recalled to court and sentenced. A breach of probation in the last month of the probationary period would expose the accused to serving the full term appropriate for the offence, notwithstanding that the accused had almost completed his probationary period.

(e) Absolute or Conditional Discharge

In 1972, the Criminal Code was amended to add an extra alternative to the range of possible sentences. When an accused pleads guilty or is found guilty of an offence for which no minimum penalty is prescribed and for which the maximum penalty is less than fourteen years, the court may, instead of convicting the accused, discharge him absolutely or on conditions prescribed in a probation order. This can be done if it is in the best interests of the accused and not contrary to the public interest. Cases have arisen where an accused foolishly commits some minor offence and finds himself in the position where the simple record of conviction will be a penalty out of all proportion to the offence. A court may now discharge the accused but it is expected that this is a power which will be used sparingly.

(f) Fine

Some offences of a minor nature contemplate only a fine, i.e., the payment of a money penalty. A short term of imprisonment is usually added in default of payment as a means of enforcing payment. For example, an accused might be sentenced to pay a fine of "$100.00 or in default 10 days". The range of fines is often prescribed in the very section that defines the offence. Sometimes a maximum only is fixed; sometimes both a maximum and a minimum is fixed. In the absence of any specific provision, a fine may be imposed in any summary conviction case as the only penalty or as a penalty in addition to any other penalty. In these cases, the fine is limited to $500 in the case of an individual and $1,000 in the case of a corporation. In indictable offences where the maximum penalty is five years or less, a fine may be imposed in lieu of or in addition to any other penalty. Where the maximum penalty is more than five years, a fine may be imposed only in addition to any other penalty. In the case of fines for indictable offences there is no maximum limit fixed. A court may direct that a fine be paid forthwith or may allow time for payment.

(g) Prohibition from Driving

When an accused is convicted of one of the offences in the Criminal Code that deals with the operation of a motor vehicle, the court may, in addition to any other penalty, make an order prohibiting the convicted person from driving a motor vehicle in Canada. The period is unlimited in the case of the most serious offences (criminal negligence causing death and manslaughter) and is limited to three years in all others. Since July of 1972 a court may restrict the operation of the prohibition to certain hours or days. An accused may now be prohibited from driving during the evening and during weekends. This change overcomes the great difficulties that were encountered in previous years where the prohibition often resulted in great hardships and the loss of employment.

Provincial legislation also provides for licence cancellations and suspensions for breaches of the driving offences in the Criminal Code as well as breaches of provincial highway traffic legislation.

CASES FOR DISCUSSION

1. Albertson, eighteen years old, obtains a job as a teller in a bank. On his nineteenth birthday, he and a group of friends celebrate freely at a tavern. Encouraged by his friends, Albertson removes the "men's washroom" sign from a door and takes it home where it is hung on the wall in his room. Several weeks later Albertson is charged with theft and pleads guilty.

> (a) As Provincial Judge faced with this situation, what would you do and why?

2. Walker was convicted of driving a motor vehicle while his ability was impaired by alcohol. The facts presented show that Walker was a truck driver. He got out of work at 4 p.m. and drank seven bottles of beer until 6:30 p.m., when he drove his car toward home. Before getting home he lost control of his car which ran up on a sidewalk narrowly missing two pedestrians and striking a storefront. Walker has a wife and four children and no previous convictions.

> (a) What penalty should be imposed and why?

3. Sykes was convicted of robbery on the basis of the following facts: About 11 p.m. Sykes entered a Joe's Milk Store which was occupied by the clerk and one customer. Sykes approached the counter where the customer was paying the clerk. He pulled out a gun and demanded money. The clerk made a move as if to resist and Sykes struck him in the face with the barrel of the pistol. He then took the money from the till, as well as money from the customer, and fled. Three days later Sykes was appre-

hended. Sykes is thirty-five and had been convicted of theft when seventeen years old and since then acquired a record of four thefts, three break and entries and two robberies. In the past eighteen years he has seldom had a job and has spent most of his time in various penal institutions. He is married and has three children but does not live with his wife and children or support them.

(a) What penalty should be imposed on Sykes and why?

4. Peters, who has dropped out of high school, is eighteen years old. He continues to live at home but is unemployed and is unable to find a steady job. He fell in with a group of other unemployed young men who persuaded him to join them in a break and entry of a warehouse. The break-in is a clumsy affair and the police, alerted by the alarm system, arrive and arrest the youths while they are carrying portable radios from the warehouse to a car. All plead guilty. Peters has no record.

(a) What penalty would you impose?

C-3

5. On August 10, 1965, at Winnipeg, Maclean was sentenced to two years in the penitentiary. On August 19, 1966, while serving the sentence at Stoney Mountain Penitentiary in Manitoba, he was injured in an accident at the prison farm. The accident occurred while Maclean was working stacking bales of straw carried up to him by a power conveyer. One of the bales struck Maclean, causing him to fall fifteen feet to a concrete floor and suffer serious injury. Maclean sued the federal government in the Exchequer Court (now Federal Court) and lost. The case was appealed to the Supreme Court of Canada and Maclean was awarded $75,000 on the grounds that the authorities were negligent in providing an unsafe system of work.

(a) Why is this case significant?

DISCUSSION

1. Periodically Parliament debates the issue of the death penalty. Should the death penalty be abolished entirely? Maintained for the few offences now covered? Extended to cover more offences? Why?

2. For approximately the past ten years, even in those cases where an accused has been sentenced to death, the federal Cabinet has always commuted the penalty to life imprisonment. Do you agree with this approach? Why or why not?

3. In *The Law in Quest of Itself,* Professor L. L. Fuller stated:
    "The Judge in deciding cases is not merely laying down a system of

minimum restraints designed to keep the bad man in check, but is in fact helping create a body of common morality which will define the good man."

4.   Do you think the sentences imposed by courts on those convicted of crimes tend to be too harsh? Too soft? Discuss.

GLOSSARY

All E. R.—All England Reports

C. R.—Criminal Reports

C. A. R.—Criminal Appeal Reports

C. R. N. S.—Criminal Reports (New Series)

O.R.—Ontario Reports

O. W. N.—Ontario Weekly Notes

O. L. R.—Ontario Law Reports

D. L. R.—Dominion Law Reports

S. C. R.—Supreme Court Reports

W.W.R.—Western Weekly Reports

Q. B. D.—Queen's Bench Division

REFERENCES TO REPORTED CASES

CHAPTER 1

C-1 *Woolmington v. The Director of Public Prosecutions,* (1935) A.C. 462 (H.L.).

C-2 *Rex v. Piggly Wiggly Canadian Limited,* (1933) 60 C.C.C. 104.

CHAPTER 2, PART TWO

C-1 *Workman v. The Queen,* [1963] 3 S.C.R. 266.

C-2 *Fisher v. The Queen,* [1961] S.C.R. 535.

C-3 *Plomp v. The Queen,* (1963) 37 A.L.J.R. 191.

C-4 *Molleur v. The King,* (1948) 98 C.C.C. 36.

C-5 *Regina v. Simmons,* (1955) 20 C.R. 223.

C-6 *Rowe v. The King,* [1951] S.C.R. 713.

C-7 *Taylor v. The King,* (1947), 89 C.C.C. 209.

C-8 *Regina v. Galgay,* [1972] O.R. 630.

C-9 *Rex v. D'Angelo,* (1927), 48 C.C.C. 127.

C-10 *Rex v. Larkin,* (1942), 29 C.A.R. 18.

C-11 *Regina v. Lamb,* (1967), 51 C.A.R. 417.

C-12 *Regina v. Judge,* (1957), 118 C.C.C. 410.

C-13 *MacTavish v. The Queen,* (1973), 20 C.R.N.S. 231.

C-14 *Regina v. Maki,* [1970] 3 O.R. 780.

C-15 *Regina v. Starrat,* [1972] 1 O.R. 227.

C-16 *Fagan v. Metropolitan Police Commission,* (1968), 52 C.A.R. 700.

C-17 *Regina v. Lascelles,* (1971), 2 C.C.C. 134.

C-18 *Lariviere v. The Queen,* (1957), 25 C.R. 279.

PART THREE

C-1 *Regina v. Wilkins,* [1964] 2 O.R. 365.

C-2 *Hibbert v. McKiernan,* [1948] 1 All E.R. 860.

C-3 *Regina v. Pearce and others,* (1852) 6 Cox Criminal Cases, 117.

C-4 *Regina v. Lieberman,* (1970) 11 C.R.N.S. 168.

C-5 *The King v. Ford,* (1970) 12 C.C.C. 555.

C-6 *Regina v. Corkum,* (1969) 7 C.R.N.S. 61.

C-7 *MacLeod v. The Queen,* (1969) 2 C.R.N.S. 342.

C-8 *Regina v. Bargiamis,* (1970) 10 C.R.N.S. 129.

C-9 *Regina v. Skivington,* (1967) 51 C.A.R. 167.

C-7　*Rex v. Henderson*, [1948] S.C.R. 226.

C-8　*Regina v. Olhauser*, (1970) 11 C.R.N.S.

C-9　*The Queen v. O'Brien*, [1954] S.C.R. 666.

C-10　*Regina v. Funnell*, [1972] 2 O.R. 301.

CHAPTER 3

C-1　*Regina v. Leech*, (1972) 10 C.C.C.

C-2　*Regina v. Quick*, (1973) 3 W.L.R. 26.

C-3　*Regina v. Aryeh*, [1972] 2 O.R. 249.

C-4　*Regina v. C.*, (1965) 53 W.W.R. 293.

C-5　*Regina v. Taylor*, (1970) 73 W.W.R. 636.

C-6　*Regina v. Dudley and Stevens*, (1884) 14 Q.B.D. 273.

CHAPTER 4

C-1　*Regina v. LeBlanc*, (1972) 8 C.C.C. 562.

C-2　*Regina v. McKibbon*, (1973) 12 C.C.C. 66.

C-3　*Rex v. Brezack*, (1949), 96 C.C.C. 97.

C-4　*Laporte v. Lagniere*, (1972), 18 C.R.N.S.

C-5　*Regina v. Ogletree*, (1972) Ontario County Court.

C-6　*Regina v. Steeves*, (1964), 1 C.C.C. 266.

CHAPTER 5

C-1　*Regina v. Smith*, (1972) 7 C.C.C. 174.

C-2　*Brosseau v. The Queen*, (1968) 5 C.R.N.S. 331.

CHAPTER 6

C-1　*Regina v. LaPierre*, (1972) 17 C.R.N.S. 247.

C-2　*Regina v. Bossence*, (1972) 16 C.R.N.S. 6.

C-3　*Maclean v. The Queen*, [1973] S.C.R. 2.

INDEX